EASY **SINGER** STYLE

pattern-free
home accents

15 easy-sew projects that build skills, too

becky hanson

Creative Publishing
international

contents

welcome to sewing!

One of the fastest and most economical ways to brighten the look of a room is to simply change its accessories. Add a decorative touch to table linens, pillows, towels, or lampshades—or create a clever wall hanging with fabrics and colors you like. *Pattern-Free Home Accents* offers you 15 projects for accessories that will help you add a personal touch to every room of your home. By combining fabrics, ribbons, decorative stitches, and threads, you'll learn to turn the simplest everyday object into something very special.

As an extra bonus, as you make these projects, you'll also be learning to sew. *Pattern-Free Home Accents* will teach you several basic sewing skills and techniques that you can use again and again. You'll be able to apply them to every type of sewing project, whether for home décor, fashion, craft sewing, or quilting.

For example, you'll learn how to create ruffles for the *Ruffle-Edge Pillow*, but you can use the same technique to add a ruffle to a slipcover or duvet. You'll learn how to do free-motion stitching when you create the *Flower Petal Table Topper*, but you can apply the same decorative technique to placemats, linens, or any other type of project. You'll learn machine appliqué, twin-needle sewing, and quilting techniques, too. Once you get some of these basic skills under your belt, the creative possibilities are endless!

Have fun! You can sew it!

fabric facts

Fabric shopping is very exciting because the options seem limitless! If you love color, texture, and design, you may find many fabrics irresistible—and you may also be tempted to buy too much of one (or more!) that you don't really need. Before you go shopping, it is important to understand some basic facts about fabrics so that you will be able to make the best choices for your projects.

Fabric Types

Not all fabrics are suitable for all projects. For example, some fabrics are soft and "drape" easily—which means they naturally fall into gentle, loose folds. Some fabrics are crisp and firm, and others have a noticeable weave or texture. The projects in this book require a range of fabrics, which will help you begin to understand the differences between them. The materials list for each project tells exactly the type of fabric that you will need.

Generally, home decorator fabrics are different from fashion fabrics, which are used to make clothing. Home décor fabrics usually have a special finish that makes them mildew resistant, stain resistant, or wrinkle resistant. They may also have more surface texture than most fashion fabrics. Chintz, moiré, sheeting, duck, sheers, and taffeta are some of the popular fabrics for home décor sewing.

Of course, you don't have to always use home décor fabrics for home décor sewing (or fashion fabrics for fashion sewing). You simply have to consider how and where you will use your finished project. For example, it would not be a good idea to make the *Patio Seat Cushion*

(page 84) out of a delicate silk moiré—even if you just love the color! Instead, you should choose a more durable fabric, such as denim, which can take the wear and tear of outdoor use. You'll find that the more you sew, the more you will be able to choose the fabrics appropriate for your project ideas—and you will also understand how the characteristics of fabrics affect the overall finished results.

Fabric Width and Length

The width of the fabric is the measurement from selvage to selvage. A selvage is the finished edge on each side of the fabric. Fabrics come in different widths, usually 36" (91.4 cm), 45" (114.3 cm), and 54" (137.2 cm), and the dimension is often displayed on the end of the fabric bolt or on a tag on a fabric roll. Most fabrics are folded on the bolt.

The length of the fabric is the measurement that runs parallel to the selvages. When you ask for an amount of fabric—for example, a yard, which equals 36" (91.4 cm)—the fabric is unrolled from the bolt, and the store clerk cuts a 36" (91.4 cm) piece for you. Your piece will be 36" (91.4 cm) long; the width will vary, depending on the width of the fabric. Most home décor fabrics are 54" (137.2 cm) wide.

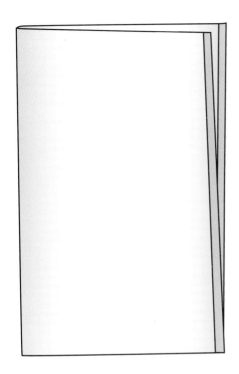

Grainlines

Fabric grain is the direction of the threads in the fabric. There is a lengthwise grain (the threads that run parallel to the selvage edges) and a crosswise grain (the threads that run perpendicular to the selvage edges). The fabric grainline affects the way a fabric drapes or moves.

The lengthwise grain is stronger than the crosswise grain. Most commercial patterns mark the direction of the grain with an arrow. When cutting out the pattern pieces, you place the arrow parallel to the lengthwise grain. The pattern piece is then positioned "with the grain," and the fabric will hang and drape correctly when your project is constructed.

Sometimes, fabrics can become "off grain" during the manufacturing process. It's a good idea to check your fabric to make sure it is straight before you begin. To check the straightness of the grain, fold your fabric from selvage to selvage. If the fabric lies flat and the selvages are parallel when folded, the fabric is straight. If it puckers or buckles at the fold line, you must straighten it. Here's how: Cut a small snip in the selvage. Then use your fingers to pull a thread across the fabric toward the other selvage edge. Pull as far as possible, then use a scissors to cut along the pulled thread. Grab the thread again, and keep pulling the thread and cutting the fabric until you reach the other selvage edge. Your fabric will now have a straight-grain edge.

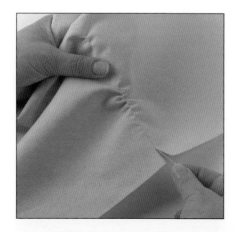

On the Bias

Another important feature of fabric is the bias. Lengthwise grain runs in one direction; crosswise grain runs in the perpendicular direction. These two straight grainlines form a 90-degree angle. Bias refers to any other angle across the surface of the fabric that is not on the straight grain. All fabric has some degree of stretch, or "give," along the bias. The maximum amount occurs when a woven fabric is cut at a 45-degree angle to the lengthwise and crosswise grain. This 45-degree angle is called true bias.

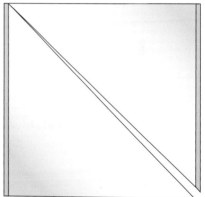

There will be times when you will want to work with fabrics cut at a 45-degree angle to the grain line—for example, when making piping for the *Pillow with Rosettes* and *Decorative Piping* (page 78). Because the 45-degree true bias allows the fabric to stretch, you can stretch the piping to fit smoothly into tight corners and curves. Piping cut on the straight grain would tend to bunch and not lie flat.

Knowing Right from Wrong

Fabrics have what is called a right side and a wrong side. The right side of the fabric is the side that, most often, appears on the outside of the project. Usually it is easy to see the difference between the right and wrong sides on fabrics like velvet or corduroy. These types of fabrics have longer threads on the right side, which create a surface texture called nap.

It's also easy to find the right and wrong sides of most cotton prints. The print is predominant on the right side of the fabric. On satins and polished cottons, the lustrous face is the right side. Sometimes the right side is obvious because of the way the fabric is woven, as in a tapestry weave or patterned brocade.

With some fabrics—plain solid cottons, for example—it can be difficult to distinguish between the right and wrong sides. In these cases, you can just choose which side of the fabric to work with as the right side. After you have cut out all the pieces for your project, mark the fabric with a safety pin, chalk marker, or piece of tape so you can identify the right and wrong sides as you sew.

Preparing Fabric for Sewing

When you're shopping for fabric, always check the end of the fabric

bolt. There you'll find information about the fabric width, but also information about the fabric's fiber content and cleaning recommendations. Keep in mind how you are going to use the finished item, and whether you prefer to hand- or machine-wash it or to dry-clean it. If you want a washable project, be sure the fabric is washable before you buy it. Some fabrics can only be dry-cleaned.

For projects that you intend to wash, you should pre-shrink the fabric before starting to sew. Pre-shrinking simply means to wash the fabric the same way you would wash the finished project. If the fabric is going to shrink at all, it will do so during the pre-washing. Also, any extra dye in the fabrics should release, so the dye won't bleed onto your finished project later.

Before washing, it's helpful to make small snips in the selvages of the fabric with your scissors, about every 3 inches (7.6 cm) or so, to keep the tightly woven selvages from drawing up along the fabric sides after washing.

If the fabric piece is large, fold it with the raw edges (not the selvages) together. Sew the ends together, with a 1/2" (1.3 cm) seam allowance (a seam allowance is the amount of fabric between your stitching line and the raw edges of the fabric). The fabric will form a large tube. The stitching keeps the fabric from becoming distorted or tangled in the washer and dryer. It also keeps the raw edges from fraying. Wash and dry the fabric and then cut off the seam. Iron the fabric, and you're ready to start.

Pressing Matters!

Pressing may feel like an unnecessary chore, but it's an essential part of the sewing process. Pressing the fabric pieces as you sew makes it easier to stitch and assemble the project and produces more professional results. It is also much easier to press fabric while it is flat rather than after the project is assembled. Get into the habit of pressing as you sew. You will enjoy the sewing process much more—and will be pleased with the results!

One of your most important tools for pressing is a good steam iron. Make sure the iron has a dependable fabric dial so you can choose the appropriate temperature for your fabrics. Some fabrics require moisture for a thorough pressing job, so you'll need to fill the iron with water to make steam. Choose a sturdy ironing board with a smooth, clean, padded surface.

The temperature of the iron should be adjusted, depending on your fabric. There are cooler settings for silk, medium settings for fabrics like wool, and hotter settings for cottons. Be sure to use the appropriate temperature so you don't scorch the fabric. Keep the surface of the iron clean at all times.

Ironing and pressing are two different techniques. Ironing is moving the iron across the fabric to remove wrinkles. Pressing is simply laying the iron down on the fabric to apply heat and pressure. You don't move the iron back and forth while it is in contact with the fab-

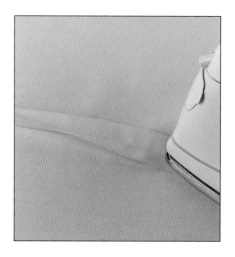

ric. You'll press to open stitched seams and fuse interfacings.

Pressing may leave a shiny mark on some fabrics, such as silk or wool, so you should work with a press cloth so that the iron does not come into direct contact with the fabric. A press cloth is a must when working with fusible interfacings in order to keep the iron and ironing board clean. Lay the press cloth over the fabric, then lay the iron on top to press. Press cloths are available at most fabric stores, usually in the section where notions are sold. You can also work with a piece of clean muslin.

tools

Here are some of the tools you'll need to make your sewing
easier and more efficient—and to produce the best possible
results. Start with these basics for measuring, marking,
cutting, and pressing. You can add more specialized tools
later as you need or want them.

Hand Needles and Pins

Make sure you have a supply of hand-sewing needles for hand stitching. Hand-sewing needles come in different sizes. The higher the number, the thinner the needle. Sizes 5 through 10 are good for general use. Purchase a package of hand-sewing needles that contains a variety of sizes, so you can experiment with what feels the best in your hand.

You will also need good-quality, sharp pins (for pinning fabrics together) and a pincushion (to keep all your pins and needles in one place!). Keep all your tools handy so that they are easy to find when you need them.

Measuring Tools

A transparent acrylic ruler usually has measurements on both sides, and some even have lines to indicate different angles, including a 45-degree angle for bias cuts. This type of ruler is a must when marking fabrics and when cutting straight lines with a rotary cutter (page 15).

Flexible tape measures are available in different lengths. The most common length is 60 inches (1.5 m), but you can also find some that measure 120 inches (3 m), which is a great size for quilting and home décor sewing. A tape measure is particularly helpful when you need to measure around curved areas.

Some tape measures are reversible, with markings on both sides: one side with imperial, or standard, measurements (inches, feet, yards) and the other side with metric measurements (millimeters, centimeters, meters).

Marking Tools

Fabric-marking tools are fast and easy to work with when marking cutting lines, sewing lines, or the position of buttons and trims. There are various types of marking tools available. Choose the one that best suits the type of fabric and the task. Read the instructions and test every marking tool on a piece of scrap before using it on your fabric.

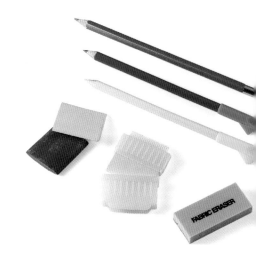

You want to be sure the marks show up clearly when you need them—and that they won't be permanent! If you are working with a fabric that needs to be dry-cleaned, it is best to use chalk markers.

Fabric-marking pens: Fabric-marking pens are quick and easy to use. Some are water-soluble, which means that you need to remove the marks with a damp cloth after you've finished sewing. Others are air-soluble, which means that they disappear on their own. Air-soluble markers are best for fabrics that show water spots when they get wet or are washed.

Chalk pencil and chalk dispensers: Chalk is great if you need to make temporary markings that you'll remove quickly—and if you are working with fabrics that need dry-cleaning. Chalk rubs off the fabric easily. Choose a color that strongly contrasts with the color of your fabric, so that it is easily visible. Chalk markers are available in lots of different colors. Some even come in a cartridge holder—much like a mechanical pencil—with a very fine point for precise marking. Chalk dispensers roll out a fine, even line of chalk. Tailor's chalk also works well and doesn't rub off as quickly as other chalk markers—but test it on your fabric first to be sure that it won't leave a mark when ironed.

Tracing wheel and paper: A tracing wheel and tracing paper are tools for marking lines on one side of a fabric. Usually, the fabric is marked on the wrong side because the marks remain on the fabric until the project is assembled and

washed. Be sure to work on a flat surface so that your markings are as accurate as possible. Choose paper of a color that contrasts well with your fabric so you can easily see the marks. Choose a wheel with either a smooth or a serrated edge, depending on the fabric you are marking. Don't press too hard when marking delicate fabrics.

Cutting Tools

High-quality cutting tools are easy to use and provide accurate results—which affects the quality of your finished work. There are many types and sizes, and each has a different use. To get started, you will need tools for cutting large fabric pieces and others for precise trimming and cutting within small areas.

Rotary cutter: Instead of cutting fabric with scissors, you can also cut it with a sharp rolling blade. Choose a rotary cutter to cut long straight edges or to cut several layers of fabric at one time. Quilters work with rotary cutters to cut many pieces at one time, quickly and easily. Replace the blade in your rotary cutter as soon as it gets dull.

You'll need three tools for rotary cutting: a cutting mat, the rotary

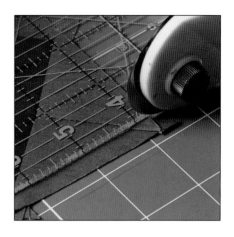

cutter, and a transparent acrylic ruler. A cutting mat is made of a special "self-healing" material that conceals the cuts. The mat also protects the top of your work surface. These three cutting tools are often sold together in kits.

Scissors: A good pair of scissors is essential to making clean, uniform cuts in your fabric. Poorly made or dull scissors will make the cutting process much more difficult—and will also produce ragged results. Scissors are available in a variety of lengths and styles, including models for left-handed sewers. Buy whichever size and style is most comfortable for you. Keep your cutting tools sharp and use them only for cutting fabrics.

Large scissors, called shears, are usually 8 to 10 inches (20.3 to 25.4 cm) long. They have a round

Machine Needles

Sewing machine needles are available in a range of sizes (or thicknesses), and the one you choose depends on the type of fabric you are sewing. Small, fine needles are best for lightweight fabrics because they won't pierce a visible hole in the fabric with each stitch. Larger needles are best for medium to heavyweight fabrics, such as denim, canvas, and upholstery fabrics. A large needle won't bend or break as easily while stitching heavy fabrics.

hole for the thumb and a larger oval to accommodate two or three fingers. Some shears have bent handles. The blade lies flat against the cutting surface as you work, which means you'll make more accurate cuts with less strain on your hands. Shears are also available with serrated edges, which grip the fabric—great when cutting knit fabrics.

Sewing scissors are about 6 inches (15 cm) long. They have two round holes for fingers, one pointed tip, and one rounded tip. The rounded tip makes it easy for you to clip and trim seams during the sewing process, because the rounded tip won't catch on the fabrics. Keep scissors and shears properly sharpened and use them only for fabric cutting.

Embroidery scissors are only about 4 inches (10 cm) long. They have very fine, sharp points, which

make them particularly good for precise trimming, cutting tight curves, and opening buttonholes. They are also handy for trimming appliqué and decorative finishing stitches.

Seam ripper: A seam ripper is small, light, and easy to handle. It's a great tool for removing basting stitches and for opening up machine-sewn buttonholes. You can also use the seam ripper to remove unwanted stitches and rip out improperly sewn seams.

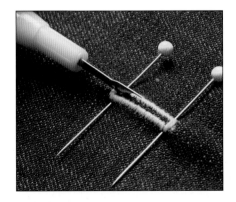

Needles are sized with numbers that indicate their thickness. The sizes are usually marked with both the metric and standard measurements. The metric number appears first. For example, a size 70/9 needle is a very thin needle— a good choice for fine or sheer fabrics. A size 90/14 is an average-size needle, good for medium-weight fabrics. Thicker needles, size 100/16 or 110/18, for example, are best for denim and other heavy fabrics.

As needles get larger in size, the eye also gets larger. If you are using a heavyweight thread, make sure the thread passes freely through the eye of the needle, so your stitching will be smooth and the needle won't break. If the thread doesn't pass freely

through the needle's eye, change to a needle that is one size larger.

Needles are also available as regular point or ball point. Regular-point needles have a sharp tip, specially designed to pierce woven fabrics. Ball-point needles, which have a round tip, are designed to sew knit and other stretch fabrics. Be sure to choose the needle that is appropriate for your fabric for the best stitch quality. Also be sure to replace a needle as soon as it becomes bent or dull or if the tip is damaged. (Check your manual for specific instructions for your machine.)

Threads

There are many different types of thread. Some are best suited for basic sewing and construction, and others are designed for decorative embellishment. There are also specific threads for topstitching and for making buttonholes. For most home décor sewing, you can thread your machine with an all-purpose thread made of cotton polyester. Most often, you'll use the same type of thread in the bobbin as you do in the needle. For decorative stitching, you can thread the needle with one of the many varieties of rayon or metallic threads, and keep an all-purpose thread in the bobbin.

For some of the projects in this book, you'll work with monofilament thread. Monofilament threads are made of nylon. They are also called invisible threads because they are clear and seem to disappear into the surface of the fabric. These threads are great for stitching trim onto a background fabric. Monofilament threads are available in two colors: clear and smoke. Clear monofilament blends best with light-colored fabrics and trims. Smoke-colored monofilament is best for darker fabrics and trims.

SINGE

EASY THREADER

AUTO
TENSION

WIDTH

S

ACCESSORIES

machine sewing

Your sewing machine is the most important and versatile tool in your sewing room. Take some time to familiarize yourself with the different parts of the machine and what they can do for you. There are many types of sewing machines available today. Some have just a handful of basic utility stitches, and some offer a larger selection of utility and decorative stitches. No matter what brand or type of machine you have, experiment with its many functions. You'll soon discover your sewing machine can help you turn all of your creative ideas into reality!

Machine Parts

Although one model may look different from another, all sewing machines work essentially the same way. If you have an instruction manual for your specific machine, spend some time reviewing it to become familiar with the specific features. Look up the basics: how to wind a bobbin, how to thread, how to solve common problems, and how to use the machine's special features.

If you don't have an instruction book, contact the manufacturer to order one. Try searching the Internet by brand name and the words "sewing machine manuals." On some sites, you can even purchase or download the manual for specific makes and models.

Hand wheel

The hand wheel is located on the right side of the machine. It allows you to manually raise the needle up and down when the machine is not running. Be sure to always turn the wheel toward you. On some machines, turning the wheel away from you may cause the threads to jam, and you'll have to rethread the machine. Get in the habit of turning the wheel toward you—it'll soon become second nature.

You will turn the hand wheel to pull up the bobbin thread before you start sewing. You will also turn the hand wheel to raise the needle to remove or reposition your fabric (for example, when finishing a seam) or to lower the needle (as when pivoting at a corner).

Presser foot, lever, and shank

The presser foot holds the fabric in place while you sew. The foot also keeps the fabric in contact with the feed dogs—the jagged "teeth" below the presser foot that move the fabric along the bed. Raise and lower the foot by lifting the presser foot lever, which is typically located on the back of the machine. The presser foot must be lowered before you sew. You raise the presser foot when threading the machine, positioning the fabric under the needle, and when changing from one style foot to another.

There are many styles of presser feet for different jobs—including a zipper foot, buttonhole foot, and satin foot (also called a special-purpose or appliqué foot). For most of your sewing, you'll use the universal, or all-purpose, presser foot. Change the presser foot by releasing the foot at the shank. On some machines, you snap the presser foot on and off the shank. On others, you release a button at the back of the shank or push up the "toes" of the foot. Check your manual for specific instructions for your machine.

Take-up lever

The top thread passes through the take-up lever, which moves up and down with the movement of the needle. (On some machines the take-up lever may not be visible.) The thread also passes through thread guides and then through the needle.

Feed dogs

The feed dogs are the rows of "teeth" that sit below the stitch plate. They help move the fabric across the plate as you sew.

At times, you may not want the feed dogs to pull the fabric through the machine—for example, when you are doing free-motion quilting (page 106). In these cases, you would cover the feed dogs with the feed dog cover plate, which snaps in place over the opening in the stitch plate.

Some machines have a drop-feed feature, a lever or switch that drops the feed dogs so they are no longer in contact with the fabric. Uncover or raise the feed dogs when you are ready to sew again in the usual way.

Needle and needle plate

Thread is threaded through the needle from front to back. When sewing, the needle passes through the stitch plate (or needle plate) and the thread loops around the bobbin thread to form stitches. The stitch plate is often marked with lines or measurements to help keep an accurate seam allowance. Precise seam allowances enable you to fit the fabric pieces together accurately.

If your machine doesn't have measured markings on the plate, you can simply measure from the needle across the plate to your desired seam allowance. For home décor projects, the seam allowance is usually ½" (1.3 cm). Mark your seam allowance guideline by placing a long piece of tape on the plate. As you sew, guide the raw edges of the fabric along the edge of the tape to maintain an even seam allowance.

Free arm

The flat bed of your sewing machine supports wide, flat sewing areas, but for sewing narrow, hard-to-reach areas, most machines also have a smaller bed called a free arm. Check your manual to learn how to convert your machine to set up for free-arm sewing as there are many styles. The free arm allows you to slide fabric all the way under and around the sewing bed of the machine. The free arm helps when sewing narrow areas (for example, a sleeve hem or the top of a drawstring bag).

Machine Controls

Different machines have different types of controls—dials, sliding levers, buttons, or touch pads—but they all allow you to adjust the basic machine settings. No matter what type of controls your machine has, here's what you need to know about what they do.

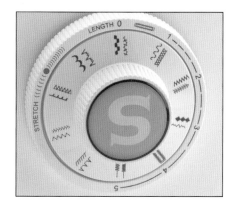

Stitch length

This control adjusts the length of the stitch. The length of the stitch you should use depends on the weight and texture of your fabric and on the type of sewing you are doing.

In general, lighter weight fabrics require a short stitch length, and heavier fabrics require a longer stitch length. For most fabrics, a good length is 10 to 15 stitches per inch (2.5 cm). Most machine manuals also have a chart indicating the stitch length for various types of fabrics.

Check the stitch length by running a few lines of stitches on a scrap piece of your fabric. If the length is too short, the fabric may pucker. Lengthen the stitch and try again, until the stitches are smooth and the fabric lies flat.

Stitch width

You change the stitch width to create various decorative effects—for example, when twin-needle stitching (page 34, step 2), or when creating satin stitch (page 44) or zigzag stitch (page 47, step 2). Some machines will automatically set the width for a decorative stitch, but experiment on a scrap piece of your fabric with different settings to see what works best for your project. Some decorative stitches require a special foot—so be sure that you are using the correct foot for the stitch you choose.

Pattern selector

The pattern selector is the control that allows you to choose the style of stitch you want to use. Depending on your machine, the pattern selector might be a dial, lever, or electronic buttons.

Machines are equipped with a variety of stitches, including utility, stretch, and decorative stitches. Utility stitches are stitches used mainly for construction, such as straight stitch, zigzag stitch, and blind hem stitch. Stretch stitches—like the over-edge stretch stitch—are designed for knit fabrics because the stitch will stretch with the fabric. Decorative stitches are designed for embellishing fabrics. Among the many types of decorative stitches are honeycomb stitch, crescent stitch, and feather stitch. Most machine manuals list all the stitch styles available on the machine.

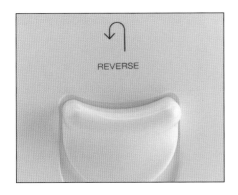

Reverse

When you use the reverse control, you sew backward to lock stitches at the beginning and end of a seam so that the seam will not come apart at the ends. Stitching in reverse is also called backstitching. Backstitching is similar to making a knot at the end of the stitching.

here's a hint!

If you need to check the presser foot pressure, "stitch" two layers of fabric (cut on the crosswise grain) without threading the machine. If the seam edges feed through the machine without shifting, the pressure is set correctly. If the seam edges are not even, adjust the pressure as needed, according to your machine's manual.

Needle position

At times, you might adjust the position of the needle to make sewing easier—for example, when installing zippers or adding piping. By moving the needle to the left or right, you can stitch more closely to the zipper or piping, for better results. Your machine may have a lever or dial to adjust the needle position to left, center, or right. On electronic machines, you can set the machine for a straight stitch and use the width control to change the position of the needle.

Presser foot pressure

The presser foot exerts pressure on the fabric while you are stitching. The amount of pressure affects the straightness of seams, the uniformity of the stitch length, and the even positioning of the layers of fabric. If the presser foot pressure is too light, the fabric will move unevenly through the machine, causing uneven seams. If the pressure is too tight, the foot can actually leave marks in the fabric.

For thin, delicate fabrics, loosen the pressure foot pressure. For heavy fabrics, like denim or canvas, increase the pressure. Check your machine manual as many machines adjust pressure automatically.

Threading

Check your machine's manual to see how to properly thread the machine. To make sure you have threaded the machine correctly, try this simple test. Thread the machine's upper thread path completely, but leave the needle unthreaded and the presser foot up. Pull the upper thread toward you—it should pull freely. Now put the presser foot down, and try pulling the needle thread again—it should resist the pulling.

If you are still able to pull the upper thread freely when the presser foot is down, the thread has not been properly threaded through the machine. Remove the thread completely and rethread, making sure the presser foot is up before you begin. After rethreading, put the presser foot down. If you feel tension when you pull the thread, you are ready to thread the needle and sew.

Stitch Tension

The stitch tension controls the upper and lower threads as they interlock to form the stitch. A perfect stitch forms when both threads are pulled into the machine with equal tension. There is no one tension setting that is best for all stitches, threads, or fabrics, so test your stitch tension before you begin your project.

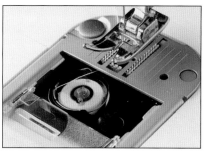

here's a hint!

For good results every time, always wind thread onto an empty bobbin. Never put thread on a bobbin that already has thread on it because it probably won't fill evenly. Also, don't over-fill your bobbin, or it won't fit properly in the bobbin case.

Sew a row of stitches on a small scrap piece of your fabric. Check to see that the threads are even on the right and wrong sides. If your stitching makes the fabric pucker, the stitch tension may be too tight. If your stitching is loopy, the stitch tension may be too loose. Try adjusting the stitch length. If that doesn't help, adjust the stitch tension with the stitch-tension control.

If you see thread accumulating on the underside of the fabric, the thread tension in the upper part of the machine is incorrect. Remove the thread from the machine and rethread it, checking the tension as described on page 23.

Bobbins

All machines form stitches by locking together two threads—a top thread and a bottom thread. The top thread comes from the spool. The bottom thread comes from the bobbin. For general sewing, use the same color thread in the spool and in the bobbin.

Each machine has its own size and style of bobbin. Wind the thread onto the bobbin with your machine's bobbin-winding mechanism. Before you begin, release the sewing action, so that when you depress the foot pedal you are winding the bobbin and not stitching. (Check your manual. Many machines release the action automatically). When the bobbin is full, place it into the bobbin case.

Depending on the machine, bobbins can be either a front-loading style or a top-loading (or drop-in) style. The bobbin case for a front-loading style bobbin is inserted into the machine under the needle plate. The bobbin case for a top-loading bobbin is inserted in front of the presser foot and covered with a removable plate. The top-loading bobbin and cover are usually transparent, so it's easy to keep track of how much thread you have left while you are sewing.

Getting Ready to Sew

Now that you have threaded the machine, practice sewing a few straight lines along the length of a scrap of fabric. Lift the presser foot and slide the fabric underneath, aligning the raw edges with the guide for the seam allowance. Make sure both the needle thread and the bobbin thread are under the presser foot and toward the back of the machine. Lower the presser foot. Sew! Watch the raw edge of the fabric rather than the needle to keep your stitching straight. When you have stitched a line of stitching, lift the needle by turning the hand wheel toward you. Then lift the presser foot to slide the fabric out.

As the machine forms stitches, the feed dogs grip and move the fabric along. Don't push or tug the fabric as you sew. Just guide the fabric as it travels beneath the presser foot. Keep a comfortable pace. You don't need to sew fast. If you are stitching too fast, you may not be able to stitch a straight line or pull out pins as you come to them. Slow down simply by easing up slightly on the foot pedal.

Never sew over a pin. When pinning the fabric, be sure all the pinheads are facing the same direction so they'll be easy for you to remove as you are sewing. The pins should be perpendicular to the line of stitching and usually about 2 to 3 inches (5 to 7 cm) apart.

As a pinned section of the fabric gets closer to the presser foot, stitch slowly so you can remove the pin—or stop stitching completely. If you hit a pin while sewing, you can damage the machine or the needle, and the broken pin pieces can cause injury. Keep a pincushion handy, and insert the pins as you remove each one.

working with the seam allowance

The seam allowance is the amount of fabric between your stitching line and the raw edges of the fabric. It's important to keep your seam allowances even and accurate so the pieces of your project will fit together correctly after they're sewn.

The size of the seam allowance depends on the project. For most home décor projects, you work with a $\frac{1}{2}$" (1.3 cm) seam allowance. For quilting, you would work with a $\frac{1}{4}$" (6 mm) seam allowance. The specific seam allowances you'll need for the projects in this book are provided with the project instructions.

While you are sewing, the lines on the stitch plate will help you maintain the seam allowance. Guide the raw edge of the fabric along the line that is marked with the measurement of the seam allowance you need. If the stitch plate is unmarked, measure from the needle with a ruler and lay a piece of colored tape on the needle plate to use as a guide.

decorative stitches and trims

Most machines have dials and settings that make it possible for you to create an inspiring mix of decorative stitches. Wondering what to do with them all?

Well, each of the projects in this chapter will teach you how to use those decorative stitches to turn everyday items into one-of-a-kind home accents. Decorative stitches add surface design without adding bulk. Don't be afraid to experiment with threads and textures once you've mastered the basics to create special effects of your own.

Topstitching

Topstitching is an easy way to add visual interest and extra strength to a project. Topstitching is usually made with a straight stitch. The stitching runs parallel to the edge of the fabric or the seam. Multiple rows of topstitching can add even more decorative detail to a simple surface, as for the *Fun Flannel Pillowcase* (page 28).

When topstitching, you will usually thread the machine with all-purpose thread. If you want to create a crisper, more well-defined edge detail, you can topstitch with two threads. Thread both threads through the machine and needle as if they were one thread. When topstitching with heavy threads or with double threads, make sure the threads move freely through the eye of the needle. If not, change to a needle that is one size larger.

Before topstitching your project, experiment with threads and stitch length on a scrap piece of your fabric until you get the look you want. (Ripping out stitches is never fun, especially when you might leave holes in the fabric!)

Twin-Needle Sewing

A twin needle consists of two needles that share a single needle shaft. When sewing with a twin needle, you can create two identical rows of stitching at the same time to produce unusual textures and designs. You can stitch with twin needles to sew hems or to create a simple decorative border or an overall pattern on the surface of your fabric, as for the *Baking-Dish Tote* (page 32).

There are various sizes of twin needle available. The most common are 2 mm, 3 mm, and 4 mm. (The measurement indicates the distance between the two needles.) Be sure that you work with a presser foot that can accommodate the extra width. Test it by turning the hand wheel slowly to make sure the needle doesn't hit the foot. If it does, set the stitch width to a narrower setting.

To thread a twin needle, thread the two threads together as one through the machine's thread path, separating them just before threading the needles. (The second spool is placed on an auxiliary spool pin. Refer to your manual.) Thread one thread through the needle on the left and the other thread through the needle on the right. Draw up the bobbin thread by turning the hand wheel toward you—just as you would if you were sewing with a single thread. Loosen the upper thread tension slightly so that the stitching will lie flat on the fabric. To create a "raised" effect with rows of texture, slightly increase the upper thread tension.

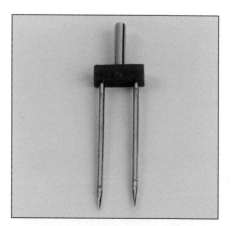

Size

19" × 32" (48.3 × 81.3 cm)

Seam Allowance

⅝" (1.6 cm)

Materials

1 yard (0.9 m) of flannel, for pillowcase body
⅓ yard (0.3 m) of flannel, for pillowcase band

Notions

Matching all-purpose thread
Contrasting rayon threads, for decorative stitching
Pins

Cutting List

From body fabric:
Cut one 27" × 42" (68.6 × 106.7 cm) piece.

From band fabric:
Cut one 11" × 42" (27.9 × 106.7 cm) rectangle
of fabric for the band.

fun flannel pillowcase

Make this cozy pillowcase as a bright room accent or maybe to take along to a slumber party. Choose kid-friendly fabrics, and make another to give away as a gift.

This pillowcase is fun and really easy to sew. Embellish the edges with rows of decorative topstitching to create a variety of styles that suit everyone's taste. You'll finish the seams with a zigzag stitch to add extra strength and durability. Pillowcases are tossed in the washing machine over and over again, so be sure to wash and dry the fabric before you cut it. There's extra fabric indicated in the materials list to allow for some shrinkage.

fun flannel pillowcase

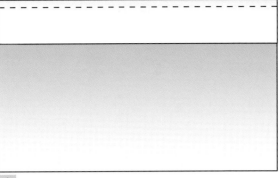

here's a hint!

Some decorative stitches—like the zigzag—are sewn with a universal foot. Other types of decorative stitches require a special foot. Check your machine's instruction manual to learn which setting you need for each decorative stitch and which foot you should use.

1 Fold and press the band fabric in half, with wrong sides together, lengthwise, to create a $5\frac{1}{2}"$ × 42" (14 × 106.7 cm) band. Pin the band to the case fabric, with right sides together, along the 42" (106.7 cm) edge, aligning the raw edges. Stitch along this edge to join the band to the case. Remember to backstitch at the beginning and end of the stitching.

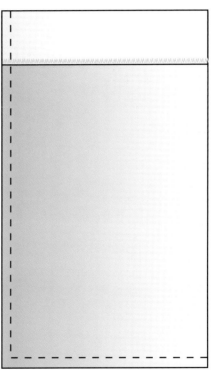

2 Change to the zigzag stitch. Align the edge of the presser foot against the raw edge as a guide and zigzag the edge. Press the seam toward the case, and press the band flat.

3 Fold the pillowcase, right sides together, matching the band seam line. Pin in place. With a straight stitch, sew the bottom and side of the pillowcase. Backstitch at the beginning and end of stitching.

4 With a zigzag stitch, sew along the side edge and bottom to keep the fabric edges from unraveling. Turn the pillowcase right side out.

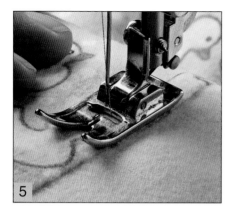

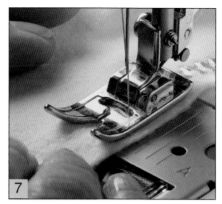

5   Working on the right side of the fabric, align the edge of the presser foot with the seam joining the band and pillowcase. Topstitch, keeping the edge the presser foot along the seam as a guide. The topstitching is not only decorative, it will hold the seam allowance of the band securely in place.

6   To stitch with two threads at once, place spools on both of the spool holders on your machine. (If your machine doesn't have a second spool holder, you can buy one.) Thread the machine with both threads as if they were one, holding the ends together. Pass both threads through the eye of the needle.

7   Line up the fold of the band under the presser foot in the desired position. In the photo above, the needle is positioned approximately $1/2$ inch (1.3 cm) from the edge of the fold. Zigzag stitch around the band. Because you are working with two threads, the stitch will look thicker than if you were working with only one. Sew multiple rows for a bolder look.

Get ready
for a sleepover!

Size

39½" × 20" (100.3 × 50.8 cm)

Seam Allowance

½" (1.3 cm)

Materials

¾ yard (0.68 m) outer fabric
¾ yard (0.68 m) lining fabric
¾ yard (0.68 m) batting
Two 13" (33 cm) wooden dowels
1 yard (0.9 m) of 1½" (3.8 cm) wide ribbon
    (for optional bow)

Notions

Fabric spray adhesive
Ruler
Marking tools
Topstitching needle (size 16 or 18)
Spool of all-purpose thread
Twin needle and second spool of thread
    (optional)
Cutting tools
Pins

Cutting List

From outer fabric:
Cut one 14" × 25" (35.6 × 63.5 cm) piece
    (referred to as the short piece).
Cut one 12" × 42" (30.5 × 106.7 cm) piece
    (referred to as the long piece).

From lining fabric:
Cut one 14" × 25" (35.6 × 63.5 cm) piece
    (referred to as the short piece).
Cut one 12" × 42" (30.5 × 106.7 cm) piece
    (referred to as the long piece).

From batting:
Cut one 14" × 25" (35.6 × 63.5 cm) piece.
Cut one 12" × 42" (30.5 × 106.7 cm) piece.

baking-dish tote

This carrier is a pretty and efficient way to carry baked treats or casseroles to parties or picnics. It closes up neatly to keep your dish warm, and the two wooden dowels make it comfortable to carry. Tie a fabric ribbon around the center, and the carrier turns into a "package" you can leave behind as a hostess gift! When opened flat, the carrier can double as a decorative table runner. The dimensions for these project instructions are for a baking dish measuring approximately 11" × 7" × 1½" (27.9 × 17.8 cm × 3.8 cm).

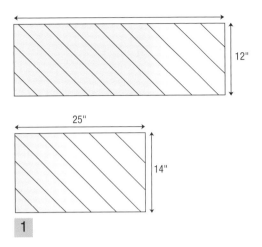

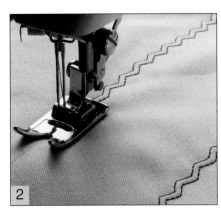

1 Following manufacturer's directions, spray the fabric adhesive on the wrong side of the batting. Join the lining pieces to the batting pieces of the same size, wrong sides together. Working with a ruler and fabric marker, draw parallel lines diagonally, about 2" (5.1 cm) apart, on the right side of the short and long lining pieces.

2 Stitch on the drawn lines, sewing through the lining fabric and batting. Working with the topstitching needle will make it easier to sew through all the thicknesses. If you want to stitch with a twin needle, remove the regular needle and replace it with the twin needle (page 27). Select a decorative stitch. (The sample in the photos is sewn with a twin-needle multistitch zigzag stitch.)

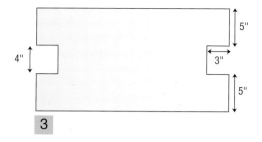

3

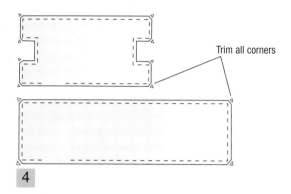

Trim all corners

4

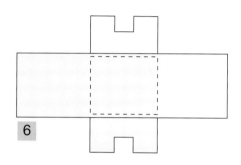

6

3 Working with the short pieces of both the lining and outer fabrics, cut out a section on each of the ends, as shown in the drawing. The cut areas should be 4" (10.2 cm) wide and 3" (7.6 cm) deep, centered 5" (12.7 cm) from the edges of the fabric. These cutout sections will help form the handles of the carrier.

4 With right sides together, pin the long lining piece to the corresponding outer piece. Do the same with the short pieces. Working with a straight stitch, stitch each of the layered pieces together with a ½" (1.3 cm) seam allowance, leaving a 4" (10.2 cm) opening along one side, as shown. The opening will allow you to turn the pieces right side out. Clip the inner corners and trim the outer corners of the seam allowance to reduce bulk.

5 Turn each piece right side out and press. Sew the openings closed either by hand or by machine.

6 Lay the two sections so that the long piece lies on top of the short one, as shown. Stitch the pieces together in the center area where they intersect.

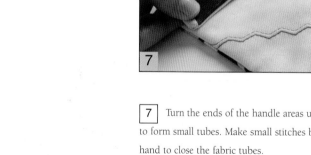

7

If you'd like, tie with a ribbon to close.

7 Turn the ends of the handle areas under to form small tubes. Make small stitches by hand to close the fabric tubes.

8 Slide the dowels into place. Insert the baking dish. Fold the fabric sections over the dish—first the long ends, and then the short ends.

Size

14" × 14" (35.6 × 35.6 cm)

Seam Allowance

½" (1.3 cm)

Fabrics

1 yard (0.9 m) 1⅝" (4.1 cm) -wide black
    organdy ribbon
½ yard (0.45 m) 1⅝" (4.1 cm) -wide gold
    organdy ribbon
1¼ yard (1.14 m) 1⅝" (4.1 cm) -wide green
    organdy ribbon
½ yard (0.45 m) white fabric

Notions

All-purpose white thread
Monofilament thread
Fabric spray adhesive
Pins
Cutting tools
Marking tools
14" × 14" (35.6 × 35.6 cm) pillow form

Cutting List

From white fabric:
Cut two 15" × 15" (38.1 × 38.1 cm) squares.
From black ribbon:
Cut two 15" (38.1 cm) pieces.
From gold ribbon:
Cut one 15" (38.1 cm) piece.
From green ribbon:
Cut three 15" (38.1 cm) pieces.

Note: Contrasting thread is used in the
photographs for visibility.

ribbon-striped pillow

Pillows are a great way to add a dash of color and texture to your home. This simple but sophisticated pillow has an easy, hand-sewn closure. Vary the colors of the organdy ribbons to make this elegant accent a perfect match for your own decor.

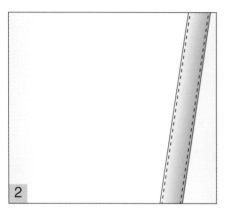

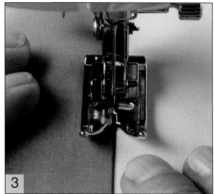

1 Wind and insert a bobbin of lightweight polycotton or cotton thread, and thread the top of the machine with the monofilament thread.

2 Spray the wrong side of the first ribbon with fabric spray adhesive, carefully following the manufacturer's directions. Position the ribbon on the right side of the white pillow front, angling it slightly, as shown in the drawing.

3 Stitch the ribbon onto the fabric by edge-stitching—which means stitching $\frac{1}{8}$" (3 mm) or less from the edge of the ribbon. Edge-stitch along both long edges of the ribbon.

fabric spray adhesive

Instead of hand- or machine-basting fabrics, you can use a fabric spray adhesive to temporarily hold fabrics together. It is easy to use and will hold trims, appliqués, and quilt layers in place until you stitch them. Follow the manufacturer's instructions for proper use, and always spray in a well-ventilated area. Don't oversaturate the fabric—just a light mist is usually enough to hold the fabric pieces together.

ribbon-striped pillow

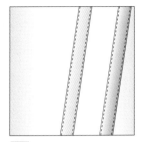 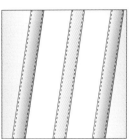 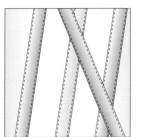 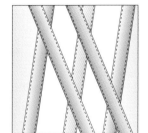 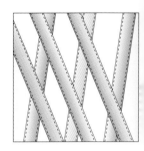

4

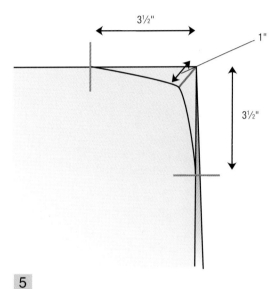

3½"

1"

3½"

5

4   Continue laying ribbons on the surface of the pillow front, as shown in the drawings. Edge-stitch each one in place after you position it.

5   Trim the pillow corners to avoid pointed "dog-ears" in the finished pillow. With right sides together, lay the pillow front on the pillow back, matching the clipped corners. Pin the pieces in place.

here's a hint!

By trimming the corners of the pillow pieces before sewing the pieces together, you will avoid creating pointy "dog-ears" on the pillow corners.

Make two marks on each side of the pillow front, 3½" (8.9 cm) from each corner, as shown in the drawing for step 5. Next, mark a point between the two marks, 1" (2.5 cm) from the tip of the corner. Connect the points by drawing lines with the fabric marker. Trim the fabric along these lines.

Repeat the process to mark and trim the remaining front corners and the corners of the pillow back.

6 Thread the needle with all-purpose thread and stitch the front and back pillow pieces, keeping a $1/2$" (1.3 cm) seam allowance. Leave a 5" (12.7 cm) opening on one side of the pillow. Slide your hand into the opening and turn the pillow cover right side out. Insert the pillow form and hand-stitch the opening to close it.

Make one or more throw pillows in a matching or complementary color scheme.

Size

10" × 12" (25.4 × 30.5 cm)

Seam Allowance

¼" (6 mm)

Materials

½ yard (0.45 m) denim for bag

6" × 6" (15.2 × 15.2 cm) bright-pink cotton
     fabric for applique

Tear-away stabilizer, enough for one 6" × 6"
     (15.2 × 15.2 cm) and one 3" × 3"
     (7.6 × 7.6 cm) piece

2½ yards (2.3 m) of ⅜" (1 cm)-wide pink satin
     ribbon for drawstring

¾ yard (0.68 m) of 1" (2.5 cm)-wide ribbon
     or bias tape for casing ribbon

¾ yard (0.68 m) ½" (1.3 cm)-wide white
     rickrack trim, cut in half

¾ yard (0.68 m) of pink satin ribbon

¾ yard (0.68 m) of white and pink
     decorative trim

Notions

Marking tools

Fabric adhesive spray

Matching all-purpose thread for construction

Contrasting rayon thread for decorative sewing

Pins

Cutting tools

Liquid seam sealant

Safety pin

Cutting List

From bag fabric:

Cut one 20" × 14" (50.8 × 35.6 cm) piece.

drawstring storage bag

You can make this bag in almost any size or shape—to stash in the closet or hang on the back of the door. Make a small bag to hold jewelry, accessories, CDs, or lingerie. Make a larger bag for shoes, pajamas, or workout clothes. The directions here are for the small, heart-appliquéd denim bag, 10" × 12" (25.4 × 30.5 cm). (The initial on the larger bag shown in the photo is also appliquéd by machine.)

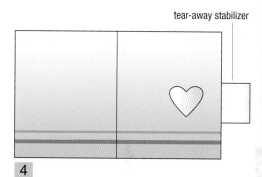

tear-away stabilizer

4

1 Fold the denim fabric in half widthwise. With a chalk marker, draw a line along the center fold. Lay the fabric horizontally in front of you, right side up. The long edge closest to you will be the bottom of the bag.

2 Working with a ruler and marking tool, now draw a series of lines along the bottom edge as guidelines for sewing on the ribbons and rickrack. Measure from the bottom edge of the fabric before you draw each line. Draw lines at $1\frac{1}{2}$" (3.8 cm), $2\frac{1}{2}$" (6.4 cm), 3" (7.6 cm), and 4" (10.2 cm) from the bottom of the fabric.

3 Work with one piece of trim at a time. Lightly spray fabric adhesive on the wrong side of each piece of trim before stitching. Place the rickrack onto the 4" (10.2 cm) line and sew it in place by stitching along its center with a straight stitch.

Choose a zigzag or another decorative stitch to sew the two ribbons. Sew one along the $2\frac{1}{2}$" (6.4 cm) line and the other along the 3" (7.6 cm) line. If you are stitching with a zigzag stitch, position the fabric so that part of the stitch falls on the ribbon and part falls onto the fabric, to enclose the raw edges. Be sure you have attached the correct presser foot for the stitches you select. Stitch another length of rickrack along the $1\frac{1}{2}$" (3.8 cm) line.

4 Working with the template (page 108), trace and cut out the appliqué shape from the cotton appliqué fabric. Spray the wrong side of the fabric with adhesive. Position the appliqué onto the denim fabric, to one side of the center fold line, as shown in the drawing.

Place the large square of tear-away stabilizer underneath the denim, directly beneath the appliqué. The stabilizer will help the fabric slide across the machine bed as you stitch.

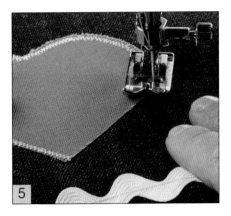

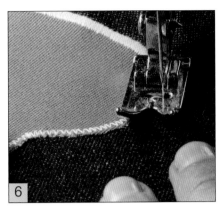

5   Zigzag-stitch around the applique, with short, narrow stitches.

6   Reposition the appliqué under the press-er foot, so that the right swing of the zigzag stitch will sew on the base fabric (denim) and the left swing will sew on the appliqué fabric. Change the settings for a short, and wider stitch and then zigzag around the appliqué again, covering the previous line of stitching. The double layer of stitching creates a smooth, slightly raised finish. Backstitch two or three stitches at the end to secure your stitching.

7   Remove the tear-away stabilizer from the back of the denim.

stabilizers

Stabilizers add support and weight to fabrics. They are helpful when machine-sewing heavy or dense decorative stitches. Stabilizers keep the fabric from buckling as it moves along the bed of the sewing machine. They also provide an extra layer of support below the stitches. You can use stabilizers as a foundation when piecing fabric and when sewing trims together. Some stabilizers—called tear-aways—are removed after stitching to reduce bulk.

There are many brands of stabilizers. Most are widely available in fabric and craft stores. Ask the clerk which type might be most suitable for your fabric and project. Always read the manufacturer's instructions, which may differ for each brand.

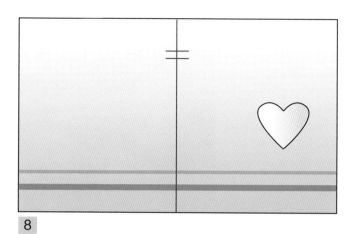

8

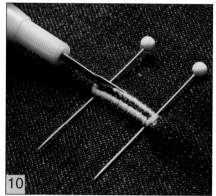

10

8 To position the buttonhole, measure from the top edge of the fabric along the center chalk line. Make a chalk mark on the center line 2¼" (5.7 cm) from the top edge. Make a second mark 3" (7.6 cm) from the top edge. These two marks indicate the top and bottom of the buttonhole. Position the 3" × 3" (7.6 × 7.6 cm) piece of tear-away stabilizer under the markings to add extra strength to the buttonhole opening.

To make the buttonhole, check your machine manual to be sure that you are using the correct foot and settings. Stitch the buttonhole.

9 Insert straight pins at the top and bottom of the buttonhole. The pins will keep you from accidentally cutting through the stitching around the buttonhole and into the fabric.

10 To open the buttonhole, insert the blade of the seam ripper (or the point of a small, sharp scissors) into the center of the buttonhole. Carefully cut toward one end of the buttonhole. Then turn the work and cut toward the other end. Strengthen the cut edges, and prevent raveling by applying liquid seam sealant to the edges (see page 86).

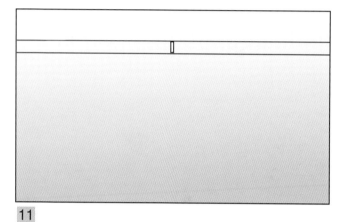

11

11 Finish the side edges of the denim fabric with tight, narrow zigzag stitches that enclose the raw edges.

The casing is a sheath that holds the drawstring in place. The casing must be wider than the ribbon drawstring so that the drawstring will move easily through the casing when you pull it. Working with a fabric pencil or chalk marker, draw a line 2¼" (5.7 cm) from the top edge, on the wrong side of the fabric. The line should sit right on the top of the buttonhole. Then draw a line 3" (7.6 cm) from the top edge, on the wrong side of the fabric. The line should sit on the bottom of the buttonhole. These two lines are the casing lines.

drawstring storage bag

11 Fold the denim fabric in half, right sides together, aligning the trims and the marks for the casing. Pin in place. With a straight stitch and a ¼" (6 mm) seam allowance, sew from the bottom of the bag to just below the bottom casing line (remember to backstitch at the beginning and end of the stitching). Do not stitch over the casing lines.

Start stitching again just above the top casing line and stitch to the top of the bag, backstitching at the beginning and end. The unstitched area between the lines forms one-half of the casing. Press open the seam above the top casing line so that it lies flat. Zigzag the edges of the seam below the bottom casing line to enclose the raw edges.

12 With a straight stitch and a ¼" (6 mm) seam allowance, stitch the bottom edge of the bag, backstitching at the beginning and end. To finish the seam, zigzag to enclose the raw edges.

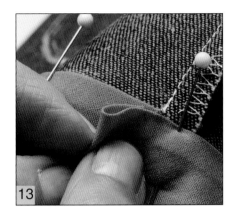

13 If your machine has a free arm, now is a good time to use it. Fold one end of the casing ribbon (or bias tape) under ½" (1.3 cm) and press. Position the casing ribbon between the drawn lines on the fabric's wrong side, tucking the raw edge of the ribbon under the folded edge. Pin in place. Edge-stitch the ribbon in place on either side, backstitching at the beginning and at the end of stitching.

here's a hint!

Satin stitching is a series of closely spaced zigzag stitches that create a smooth satinlike surface. You can satin-stitch monograms or appliqués. Always try a sample on a scrap of your fabric first, to get the stitch just the way you like it. The stitches should be close enough that no fabric shows between them, but not so close together that the fabric and stitches don't feed under the foot. Check your instruction manual for the settings and the proper foot for creating the satin stitch.

14 To hem the top edge of the bag, press the edge 1/4" (6 mm) toward the wrong side of the bag. Stitch down the fold. Turn over the edge again and press it in place. Pin and topstitch all around the fabric. Backstitch at the beginning and end of stitching.

15 Cut the drawstring ribbon into two equal pieces. Fold over the end of one piece of ribbon and insert a safety pin through it. Close the pin. Push the pin through the buttonhole and into the casing. Work the pin through the casing, around the bag, and out again through the buttonhole. Remove the safety pin and attach it to the folded end of the second piece of ribbon. Thread this ribbon through the casing the same way, starting on the opposite side. Knot the ends of the ribbons—add a bead if you'd like.

Tie the ribbons into a bow to hang the bag onto a peg or hook.

Size

Hand towel 2" × 20" (5.1 × 40.6 cm)
Bath towel 2" × 30" (5.1 × 76.2 cm)

Seam Allowance

½" (1.3 cm)

Materials

One sage green hand towel
One sage green bath towel
4 yards (3.66 m) of ⅞" (2.2 cm)-wide celery
    green satin ribbon
4 yards (3.66 m) of ¼" (6 mm)-wide rose
    satin ribbon
4 yards (3.66 m) of ⅜" (1 cm)-wide patterned
    ivory ribbon
1 yard (0.9 m) or 1 package of lightweight
    tear-away stabilizer

Notions

Tape measure
Rayon threads for decorative stitching
All-purpose thread to match widest ribbon
Monofilament thread
Pins

Cutting List

Measure the short side of the bath towel and add
3" (7.6 cm). The total is your bath towel measurement. Measure the short side of the hand
towel and add 3" (7.6 cm). The total is your
hand towel measurement.

For stabilizer:
Cut one piece 3" (7.6 cm) wide by [bath towel
    measurement].
Cut one piece 3" (7.6 cm) wide by [hand towel
    measurement].

For green ribbon:
Cut one piece equal to [bath towel measurement].
Cut one piece equal to [hand towel measurement].

For rose and ivory ribbons:
Cut two pieces equal to [bath towel measurement].
Cut two pieces equal to [hand towel measurement].

Note: Contrasting thread is used in the
photographs for visibility.

decorator towels

Add a splash to your bath with these stylish towels—which you can make in a flash! Sew a few satin ribbons together on a foundation stabilizer to create a ribbon "band." Then stitch the band to the surface of the towel. That's it! You can use the same technique to add ribbons and trims to window treatments and shower curtains, too. Follow these directions to make one bath towel and one hand towel.

1   Thread the needle with the green rayon thread. Wind the bobbin with the all-purpose ivory thread. Choose the decorative stitch you would like to stitch on the surface of the green ribbon (a honeycomb stitch was used on these towels).

Before you actually stitch on the ribbon, test the effect on a scrap piece of your fabric or ribbon to be sure you like the look. Be sure you have the proper foot for the stitch you choose. When you've selected your decorative stitch, position the green ribbon in the center of the stabilizer. Stitch the ribbon to the stabilizer.

2   Next, lay one rose ribbon alongside the green ribbon, so that the long edges meet but do not overlap. With monofilament or a matching thread and a wide zigzag stitch, stitch the rose ribbons to the stabilizer. The zigzag stitch should be wide enough to just "bite into" both the green and rose ribbons to connect them. Stitch the other rose ribbon to the other side of the green ribbon the same way.

here's a hint!

Make both towels at the same time. Complete a step for one towel, then repeat the step for the other. This method of working is quicker and easier than completing the towels one at a time, because you will need to change stitches and threads in different steps of the process.

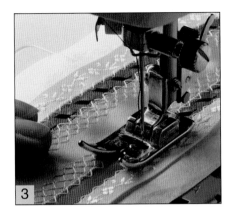

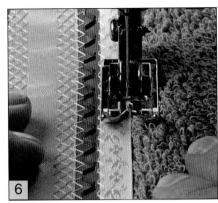

3   Now position the ivory ribbons on either side of the rose ribbons, so that the edges meet but do not overlap. With monofilament or matching thread, zigzag-stitch the ivory ribbons alongside the rose ribbons in the same way.

4   For a richer texture, choose a contrasting-color thread, widen the zigzag stitch, or select another decorative stitch to stitch along the center of the rose ribbons.

5   Trim away the excess stabilizer. Press lightly. Position the ribbon band over the band area of the towel. The ribbon band will be longer than the towel. Pin in place.

6   With ivory thread and a medium-length straight stitch, carefully stitch the ribbon band to the towel. Stitch one side of the band at a time, sewing right along the edge. (To make the stitching easier, try using the zipper foot. Change the needle position as necessary.)

here's a hint!

Monofilament thread is nylon, and the ribbons are delicate, so be sure to use a cool setting on your iron when pressing so the threads and ribbons aren't damaged. Thread the monofilament through the needle, but use a lightweight polyester-cotton or cotton thread in the bobbin.

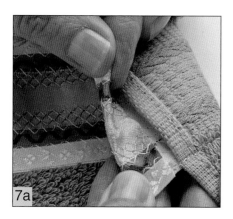

7 Fold under ½" (1.3 cm) of the raw edge of the ribbon band at each end. Fold the band again to the back of the towel, enclosing the finished edge of the towel. Stitch close to the folded edge of each ribbon to finish.

Display your
towels on a
decorative rack.

surface design and texture

Your sewing machine probably has lots of stitching options that go way beyond the basics of straight stitch, zigzag, and over-edge. But what to do with all those fancy stitches? With a little imagination, you can mix and match stitches, ribbons, and threads to create one-of-a-kind designs and textures for your projects. Here are just a few ideas to get you started. After you've had a peek at what's possible, you'll be ready to discover many more ideas on your own.

Reverse Bobbin Work

With reverse bobbin work, you actually sew the project with the right side down. You also stitch with a heavy thread or narrow ribbon in the bobbin. When you've finished stitching, you have a thick, textured stitch on the right side of the fabric. You won't believe how beautiful and easy this special effect is! Try this technique with rayon floss, lightweight crochet cotton, or 2 mm silk ribbon.

Thread the needle with all-purpose thread in a color that matches the "thread" on the bobbin (rayon threads are not strong enough for this technique and monofilaments may cause puckering). Select a stitch that is fairly open rather than a dense one that requires stitching several times in the same area, or the bottom thread may jam. Some stitches that work well are zigzag, serpentine, vine, and feather stitches. Explore and experiment to find the ones you like.

For reverse bobbin work, you wind the bobbin with heavy thread or silk ribbon, either by hand or by machine. If you are winding by machine, wind the thread or ribbon just as you would any other bobbin thread.

Couching

Couching is the process of stitching over ribbons, trims, or cords to attach them to the right side of the fabric. This technique produces interesting three-dimensional textures. Completely cover the surface with couching—as for the *Fancy-Stitch Pillow* (page 56)—or simply create a dramatic, decorative border.

Some machines have a foot that serves multiple purposes, including couching. For heavy or heavily textured trims, you might want to try a satin (or appliqué) foot, a cording foot, or open-toe foot. Some cording feet have grooves, holes, or openings that allow yarns or cords to travel smoothly under the foot as you stitch over them.

Choose monofilament, matching, or contrasting threads to create varied effects. You can also couch with many styles of decorative stitches, depending on the type of ribbon, trim, or cord you are working with. Draw a chalk line in advance and follow the line as you stitch—or just stitch in a random pattern.

Experiment with narrow ribbons, thin fabric strips, crochet or pearl cottons, and even yarns.

Piecing

Piecing irregular shapes together with decorative stitches is a technique sometimes called crazy quilting. First you position different types of irregularly cut fabrics onto a foundation fabric (such as muslin). Then you stitch them in place with a variety of decorative stitches. Choose a specific color palate or use several colors of fabrics and threads. You can even mix fabrics—pairing cotton and velveteen with silk and satin, for example. Piecing is a great way to use up your fabric scraps!

Don't be afraid to experiment with stitches and different weights of thread. Stitch onto ribbons or try out a twin needle (page 27). When you've finished, turn your pieced fabric into a quilt, pillow front, or *Crazy Quilt Lampshade* (page 60). Try piecing small sections of a project, too—the border of a table runner or the edge of a pillowcase. Piecing is a great technique for new sewers because you just make up the design as you go!

Size
Placemat 19" × 14" (48.3 × 35.6 cm)
Napkin 16" × 16" (40.6 × 40.6 cm),
Napkin ring 2⅛" × 6" (5.3 × 15.2 cm)

Seam Allowance
½" (1.3 cm)

Materials
½ yard (0.45 m) of fusible interfacing
½ yard (0.45 m) of linen for placemat
        and napkin ring
½ yard (0.45 m) of cotton or linen for napkin

Notions
Ruler
Marking tools
All-purpose thread to match fabric
2 mm-wide silk ribbon
All-purpose thread to match ribbon
Pins
Hand-sewing needle with large eye

Cutting List
From placemat/napkin ring fabric:
Cut two 16" × 21" (40.6 × 53.3 cm) pieces
        for placemat.
Cut one 5" × 6" (12.7 × 15.2 cm) piece
        for napkin ring.
From fusible interfacing:
Cut one 16" × 21" (40.6 × 53.3 cm) piece.
Cut one 5" × 6" (12.7 × 15.2 cm) piece.
From napkin fabric:
Cut one 18" × 18" (45.7 × 45.7 cm) square
        for the napkin.

placemat, napkin, and napkin ring

You can custom-design decorative place settings—placemats, napkins, and napkin rings—both for everyday dining and for special occasions. You can also make sets to give as housewarming, shower, or hostess gifts. These chocolate-brown placemats have several rows of decorative blue stitching created with reverse bobbin work. A very narrow silk ribbon is wound in the bobbin, and the project is sewn with the wrong side of the fabric facing up—so the bold, beautiful texture appears on the right side, just below the diner's plate! With these instructions, you'll make one of each item.

If you are making more than one placemat, to save time, repeat each step for each placemat before moving on to the next step. Do the same when making multiple napkin rings and napkins.

The Placemat

1 Fuse the interfacing to the wrong side of one of the 16" × 21" (40.6 × 53.3 cm) linen pieces, following the manufacturer's instructions.

2 Lay the linen, interfacing side face up, on a flat surface. Working with a ruler and a fabric marker or chalk, mark a stitching line 1" (2.5 cm) in from all four edges, as shown in the drawing. Mark another stitching line 3½" (8.9 cm) in from all four edges. (The area between the stitching lines is the border area.)

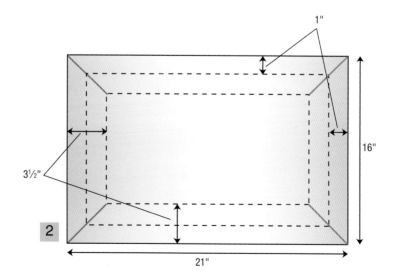

Mark a diagonal line from the corners of the inside rectangle to the corners of the fabric. These lines will be your stitching guide as you sew and pivot at the corners.

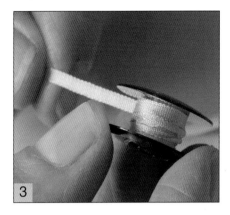

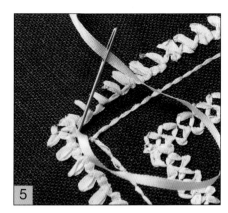

3 Wind the bobbin with the silk ribbon by hand or machine (page 50). Thread the needle with an all-purpose thread that matches the color of the silk ribbon.

4 Position the fabric under the needle, wrong side up. The interfacing will be facing you as you stitch. Select a decorative stitch and the proper foot. Fill the border area with rows of decorative stitching. Leave thread and ribbon tails about 4" (10 cm) long at the beginning and ending of the stitching.

5 When the stitching is finished, thread the ribbon through the eye of a large hand-sewing needle.

6 Bring the tails through to the wrong side of the fabric and tie the ends together.

7 Rethread the needle and the bobbin with thread that matches the fabric. Set your machine for a straight stitch. With right sides together, pin together the front and back pieces of the placemat. Stitch, with a $1/2$" (1.3 cm) seam allowance, leaving a 5" (12.7 cm) opening on one side. Trim the corners, turn the placemat right sides out, and press. Hand-stitch the opening closed.

ribbon in the bobbin

If your machine has a front-loading bobbin, you may have to loosen the bobbin tension screw before you wind the bobbin with ribbon or heavy thread. If your machine has a "drop-in" (top loading) style of bobbin, you can either thread the ribbon as usual into the bobbin case, feeding it through the tension slot, or you can bypass the tension slot altogether. If you bypass the slot, the finished stitch will have a more relaxed appearance, as you see in the top row of stitching. If you thread the ribbon into the slot, the finished stitch will have a tighter appearance (as in the bottom row). Experiment to see what effect works best for your project.

8 Lay the placemat, right side up, on a flat surface. With a chalk marker, draw a box inside the border area, about 3¼" (8.3 cm) from the outside edges. Draw diagonal lines about 1½" (3.8 cm) apart inside the box, in both directions, as shown in the drawing. Set your machine for a long stitch length, and stitch along the diagonal lines, backstitching at the beginning and end of each row.

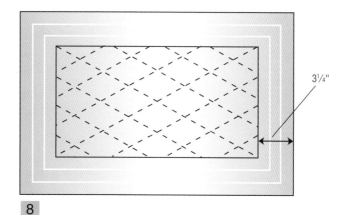

3¼"

8

The Napkin Ring

1 Fuse the small piece of interfacing to the wrong side of the 5" × 6" (12.7 × 15.2 cm) piece of linen. Mark a line 1¾" (4.5 cm) from each long edge. Wrong side up, sew rows of reverse bobbin stitching within the lines to match the placemat, as in step 4 on page 54.

2 With right sides together, fold the fabric in half lengthwise and pin along the long edge. With all-purpose thread in the machine and bobbin, stitch the edge with a ¼" (6 mm) seam allowance. Turn right sides out.

3 Press under ¼" (6 mm) of the fabric around one open end. Tuck the other end into the pressed end, overlapping about ¼" (6 mm).

4 Hand-stitch the napkin ring closed.

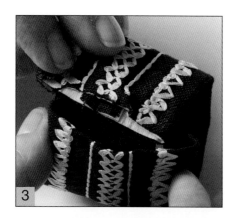

3

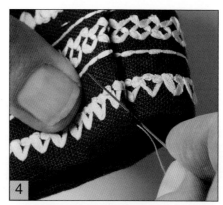

4

The Napkin

1 Press under ⅜" (1 cm) along each edge of the 18" (45.7 cm) cotton square. Press the edge under again.

2 Stitch the folded edge with a straight stitch and matching thread.

You're all set to set your table!

here's a hint!

If the bobbin should run out of ribbon while you are in the middle of the stitch, bring the ribbon tail through to the wrong side of the fabric. Start the stitching again with a full bobbin, then tie the ribbon tails together.

Size
14" (35.6 cm) square

Seam Allowance
¼" (6 mm) and ½" (1.3 cm)

Materials
⅛ yard (0.11 m) of chocolate-brown
    silk dupioni
⅔ yard (0.6 m) of copper silk dupioni
⅛ yard (0.11 m) of turquoise silk dupioni
¼ yard (0.23 m) of fusible interfacing
1⅛ yard (1.03 m) of ½" (1.3 cm)-wide turquoise
    satin ribbon
1⅛ yard (1.03 m) of 1" (2.5 cm)-wide
    brocade trim
1¾ yard (1.6 m) of fringed trim

Notions
Matching all purpose thread
Pins
Rayon thread for decorative sewing
    (chocolate brown, turquoise)
Pearl crown rayon or crochet thread for
    decorative sewing (chocolate brown,
    copper, and/or turquoise)
Cutting tools
14" (35.6 cm) square pillow form

Cutting List
From the copper silk:
Cut one 15" × 15" (38.1 × 38.1 cm) square
    for pillow back plus one piece 3½" × 37"
    (8.9 × 94 cm).
From the turquoise and chocolate-brown silk:
Cut one piece each 4" × 37" (10.2 × 94 cm).
From the interfacing:
Cut one piece 9" × 37" (22.9 × 94 cm)

fancy-stitch pillow

Bring together all the colors of a room with one perfect accent. This bold, textured pillow is a canvas full of ribbons, trims, threads, couching, and decorative machine stitching. Create unique effects by varying the widths of the ribbons and fabric strips. Try combining different fabrics and textures—like velvet, silk, and satin. Contrasting colors will create drama, and more harmonious colors create sophistication. You'll be surprised how easy it is to create this dazzling look!

1 | Thread the machine and bobbin with all-purpose thread. Pin a long edge of the chocolate-brown silk strip to a long edge of the copper silk strip, right sides together. Sew, leaving a 1/4" (6 mm) seam allowance. Press open the seam.

2 | With right sides together, pin the turquoise silk strip to the other long edge of the copper strip. Sew and press open the seam. Fuse the interfacing to the wrong side of the pieced strips, following the manufacturer's instructions.

3 | With a straight stitch, stitch the brocade trim along the seamline of the chocolate and copper strips.

here's a hint!

Work with special presser feet to stitch novelty threads onto the surface of the fabric. The satin foot (also called a special-purpose foot) has a grooved bottom that allows thick or heavy threads to pass underneath easily. A cording foot has holes or slots on top of it, through which you can place one, two, or three strands of cord. Experiment with ribbon floss, lightweight yarns, crochet cotton, and other textured strands.

fancy-stitch pillow

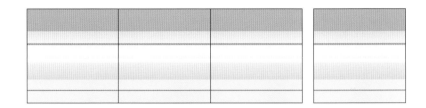

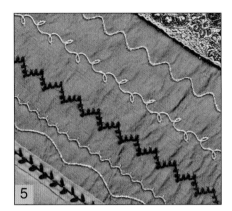

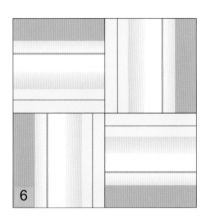

4 | Choose a decorative stitch and a contrasting or matching thread color. Sew the turquoise satin ribbon onto the chocolate-brown strip.

5 | Embellish the surface of the fabrics with couched cords (page 51) and with a variety of decorative thread colors and stitches—zigzag, thorn, chevron, honeycomb, to name a few of the many choices.

6 | Cut the embellished strip into four 8" × 8" (20.3 × 20.3 cm) squares. Rotate the squares to form a larger square, as shown in the drawing. With a straight stitch, sew the squares together with a ½" (1.3 cm) seam allowance. Press open the seams.

here's a hint!

To add dimension to your stitching, try winding pearl crown rayon onto the bobbin. Select a decorative stitch—a wide zigzag, for example. Turn the fabric face down and stitch. The bobbin thread stitches on the right side of the fabric, adding texture and interest to the surface.

Your fancy new pillow will transform the room.

7 Pin the trim to the outside edges of the pillow top, positioning the edge of the trim within the seam allowance. Be sure that you are pinning the trim to the right side of the pillow top. Straight-stitch the trim in place with a $1/2$" (1.3 cm) seam allowance.

8 Pin the pillow back to the pillow front, right sides together. Stitch with a $1/2$" (1.3 cm) seam allowance, backstitching at the beginning and end. Leave a 5" (12.7 cm) opening on one side of the pillow. Turn the fabrics right side out. Insert the pillow form. Hand-sew the opening closed.

Size

Bottom diameter 11" (27.9 cm)

Top diameter 4" (10.2 cm)

7" High (17.8 cm)

Materials

$\frac{1}{2}$ yard (0.45 m) of muslin

Cotton fabric scraps, cut into different shapes
    to create interest

Trim for the lampshade's top and bottom
    (measure the circumferences to be sure you
    buy enough)

$\frac{1}{2}$" (1.3 cm) wide satin ribbon, to finish
    the inside raw edges of the lampshade
    (buy the same amount of ribbon as trim)

Notions

One self-adhesive lampshade

Marking tools

Ruler

Cutting tools

All-purpose threads that contrast with the
    fabric scraps

Craft glue

crazy quilt lampshade

Turn a small table lamp into a work of art by making
your own crazy lampshade. This colorful pieced project
allows you to use up your favorite fabric scraps—while
you let your imagination run wild! Purchase a self-
adhesive lampshade, piece your fabrics, and glue on
the trim. It's easy and fun. This lampshade will brighten
any room—and will let your personal style shine
through.

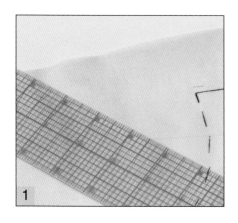

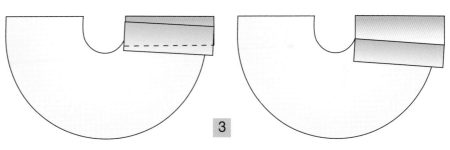

1 Remove the paper label from the lampshade. You will use the label as a template.
Lay the template on the muslin. Working with
a marker and transparent ruler, transfer the
shape of the template onto the fabric, adding
1" (2.5 cm) all around for seam allowances.

2 Cut the muslin along the drawn lines.
You will sew the fabric scraps directly onto the
muslin. The foundation of muslin makes it
easier to piece the odd shapes and also helps
the stitched fabrics hold their shape.

3 Lay a scrap of one of the cotton fabrics
on one end of the muslin, right side up, so
that it overlaps the edge of the muslin, as
shown in the drawing on the left. Lay another
scrap of a different cotton fabric wrong side up
on top of the first, with the raw edges together.
Stitch the two scraps together with a ¼" (6
mm) seam allowance. Flip the second piece
over to the right side as shown in the drawing
on the right. Press.

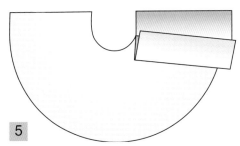

4 Choose a decorative stitch and contrasting thread. (Be sure that you attach the proper foot for your stitch, if necessary.) Working on the right side of the fabric, stitch over or close to the seam you just made.

5 Lay a third fabric scrap, right side down, onto the right side of second piece, raw edges together, as shown in the drawing. Position the third scrap at a slight angle. Straight-stitch with a 1/4" (6 mm) seam allowance. Flip the third piece over to the right side. Press and sew with a decorative stitch.

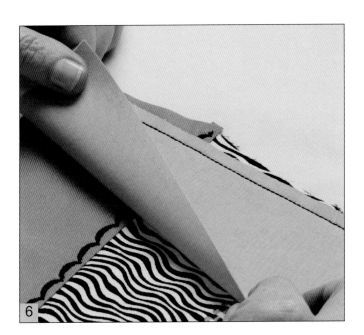

6 Continue to add fabric scraps in this way until you have covered all of the muslin. Be sure to position each fabric scrap so that all the raw edges of the muslin and the scraps will be covered when the scraps are flipped over to the right side. Some pieces may overlap—which is fine and actually is unavoidable when working with varied sizes and shapes.

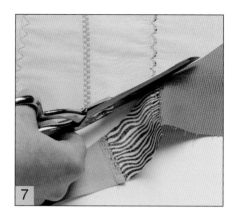

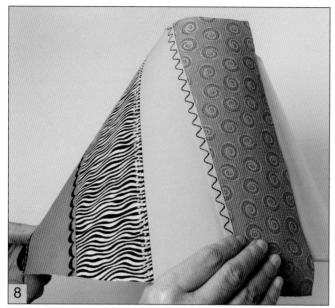

7 To finish the lampshade, turn the fabric right side down, so that the muslin foundation is facing you. Cut the excess scrap fabrics away from the edges of the muslin.

8 Carefully follow the lampshade manufacturer's directions to apply the fabric/muslin piece smoothly to the sticky surface of the lampshade. Take your time!

9 Turn the edges of the fabric piece to the inside edges of the bottom of the lampshade and glue them in place with craft glue. Glue the ½" (1.3 cm) satin ribbon over the raw edges inside the shade.

10 Glue decorative trim to the top and bottom edges of the lampshade to add your finishing touch!

Flip the lightswitch
    to get the full effect!

gathering

Ruffles add a frilly, vintage touch to any type of project. In home décor, ruffles are often added to the bottom of curtain valences, round tablecloths, and the edges of pillows or pillow shams. No matter what type of project you are making, you create ruffles simply by gathering fabric.

There are two ways to gather fabric on the machine. For lightweight fabrics, such as sheers and lace, you gather the fabric by sewing two rows of stitches and then pulling the threads. For heavy fabrics, such as taffeta and denim, you gather the fabric with cord.

The type of fabric determines how much you need to gather it, too. Lightweight fabrics can be gathered more densely to create a full ruffle. Heavier fabrics are gathered a bit more loosely to create a deep, gentle wave.

Gathering with Stitching

To gather lightweight fabrics, set your machine to the longest (basting) stitch and loosen the upper thread tension. Thread the bobbin with a heavy thread, such as a buttonhole twist. Sew two rows of stitching within the seam allowance of the ruffle. Do not backstitch or cross the lines of stitching. When finished, pull the bobbin threads to create the ruffles. Adjust the fullness so the gathers are evenly distributed. The gathered fabric is now ready to be sewn into the project.

Gathering with Cord

To gather heavy fabrics, sew a wide zigzag stitch over a cord or heavy thread. Hold a 4" (10.2 cm) thread tail at the back of the machine as you start to sew. Don't catch the cord or heavy thread in the zigzag stitches. The stitching forms a channel for the cord, which the cord slides through as you pull it to create gathers. Pin the gathered fabric in place and pull the cord to form the ruffles. This method can also be used to create fabric rosettes, as for the pillow on page 78.

Gathering Lace

The *Scented Sachet* (page 66) is trimmed with gathered lace. Some laces are already gathered when you buy them; others you need to gather yourself. If your lace is 100 percent cotton, it will probably have a "gathering thread" in the finished heading. This thread is usually the top thread of all the threads in the straight part of the lace heading. Simply pull the thread to create gathers.

If your lace is not cotton or does not have a gathering thread, you can gather it by hand with a needle and thread. Sew a long stitch through the lace heading, and then gently pull the thread to gather the lace.

Gather the lace slightly for a more delicate look, such as at the bottom edge of a curtain valence. Gather tightly if you want a fuller look, as for the *Scented Sachet*.

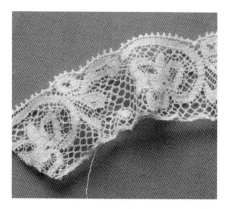

Size
4" (10.2 cm) sq.

Materials
Two 5" × 5" (12.7 × 12.7 cm) squares of
 dupioni silk
¼ yard (0.23 m) of insertion lace
 (a flat lace with a finished edge on
 both sides)
½ yard (0.45 m) of double-sided flat
 eyelet lace
⅔ yard (0.6 m) of gathered lace (see page 65)
½ yard (0.45 m) of ¼" (6 mm) wide satin
 ribbon

Notions
Marking tools
Pins
Tapestry needle or bodkin
All-purpose thread (matching the lace and silk)
Rotary cutting tools
Fiberfill
Potpourri in your favorite scent

Note: Contrasting thread is used in the
photographs for visibility.

scented sachet

This vintage-style scented sachet is the perfect size to tuck in a drawer of linens or lingerie. But it's so pretty you might not want to hide it away. Display it on top of a bedroom dresser or on a bathroom vanity. Or hang it from a ribbon on a closet door to catch a faint hint of your favorite scent each time you open the door.

This lacy sachet is made with silk dupioni, but you can substitute cotton or any other tightly woven fabric. Choose fabrics and laces in similar shades to create a monochromatic look, or choose contrasting colors for a bolder effect. Experiment with different shapes, too—perhaps a rectangle or circle. Make two or more of these little sachets—at least one for yourself and one for a friend.

1   With a fabric pencil or chalk marker and a ruler, mark a diagonal line from corner to corner on the right side of one of the silk squares. Mark another line 1/2" (1.3 cm) away from each side of the center line.

2   Pin a piece of the eyelet lace on the square, aligning its edge along one of the outer lines. Position the lace so it does not cover the other two lines. Stitch the edges of the lace with a narrow zigzag stitch. Keep the edge of the lace centered under the presser foot so that the zigzag swings evenly from the fabric to the lace surfaces. (You will trim the excess lace overhanging the edges of the square later.)

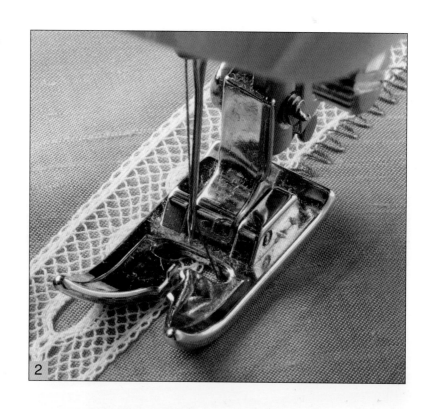

scented sachet

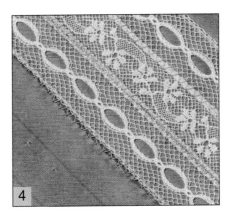

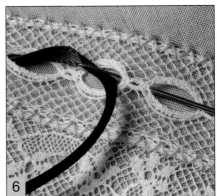

3 Working away from the center line, position a piece of insertion lace next to the eyelet lace so that their edges meet. Pin in place. Stitch the insertion lace to the eyelet lace with a narrow zigzag stitch, as before.

4 Pin another piece of the eyelet lace alongside the insertion lace. Zigzag-stitch in place.

5 Repeat steps 2 through 4 on the other side of the fabric square, aligning the edge of the first piece of eyelet with the outer line.

6 Thread the satin ribbon through the eye of a tapestry needle. Then thread the ribbon through the holes in the eyelet lace strips.

7 You can also weave the ribbon through the eyelet with a special tool called a bodkin.

here's a hint!

Basting is a type of temporary stitching that holds fabric pieces in position as you sew the permanent lines of stitching. If you are basting by machine, use your machine's longest stitch setting and loosen the tension so that the stitches are easier to remove.

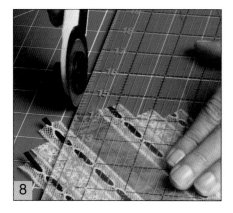

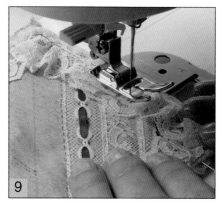

8 Straight-stitch around the edges of the square, with a scant ¼" (6 mm) seam allowance, to attach the ribbon and lace to the fabric edges. Working with a rotary cutter (page 15), trim the excess ends of the lace so that they are even with the raw edges of the fabric square. Trim the fabric on all four sides of the square.

9 With right sides together, pin the gathered lace to the edges of the square. Align the gathered edge of the lace with the raw edge of fabric. Adjust the gathers so that they are evenly distributed around all four sides of the square.

Stitch the lace to the fabric with a long, basting stitch and a scant ¼" (6 mm) seam allowance. Pin the two fabric squares, right sides together.

10 Be sure the gathered lace is sandwiched between the two squares. Set the machine to a normal stitch length. With a ¼" (6 mm) seam allowance, stitch around the sachet, pivoting at the corners. Leave a 2" (5.1 cm) opening on one side. Carefully turn the fabrics right side out. Stuff the sachet with potpourri and fiberfill. Hand-sew the opening to close.

Tuck the sachet
in a drawer
you open often!

here's a hint!

You can use vintage lace for this project—or you can give brand-new white lace a vintage look. Just brew some strong tea and let it cool. Place the lace in the tea and let it soak. Check periodically to see if the color is as dark as you'd like it to be. (Remember, wet fabric and lace will appear darker when wet.) Rinse the lace, let it dry, and then press. Your tea-dyed "vintage" lace is ready to sew!

Size

14" (35.6 cm) square

Materials

1½ yards (1.37 m) of fabric for pillow front,
    back, and ruffle
One 12" (30.5 cm) zipper (to match
    fabric color)

Notions

Marking tools

Pins

Matching all-purpose thread

Lightweight cord or heavy thread

Glue stick (optional)

One 14" (35.6 cm) square pillow form

Cutting List

Cut one 15" × 15" (38.1 × 38.1 cm) square
    for pillow front.
Cut two 8½" × 15" (21.6 × 38.1 cm) pieces
    for pillow back.
Cut 120" (3 m) of 6' (15.2 cm) wide
    bias strips to make the ruffle.

Note: Contrasting thread is used in the
photographs for visibility. Construct the project
with matching thread.

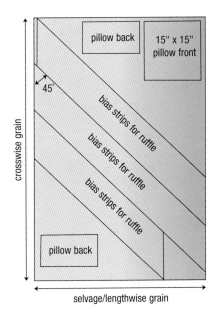

ruffle-edge pillow

A ruffle can really enhance the look of a pillow—whether the fabric is a casual cotton calico or a sophisticated, shimmering taffeta. This project features a ruffle gathered with the cording technique, which works best with a firm fabric. The pillow also has a zipper at the back, which makes the pillow cover easy to remove to wash or dry-clean.

Inserting the Zipper

1 Place the two pillow back pieces right sides together. With a fabric pencil or chalk marker, draw a line along the length of the fabric, 1" (2.5 cm) from the long raw edge. Make a mark 1½" (3.8 cm) from the top of the line and another mark 1½" (3.8 cm) from the bottom. Pin along the marked line.

2 Sew from the bottom of the fabric until you reach the first 1½" (3.8 cm) mark, back-stitching at the beginning and end of the stitching. Reposition the fabric and sew from the second mark to the top of the fabric, backstitching at the beginning and end.

3 Change the stitch length to the longest stitch (or basting stitch). Machine-baste the unstitched portion of the line. Press open the basted seam.

4 Open the zipper and place it face down on the seam allowance, centered over the basting stitches. The coil of the zipper should rest on the seam line. Attach the right side of the zipper to the seam allowance with pins or a glue stick.

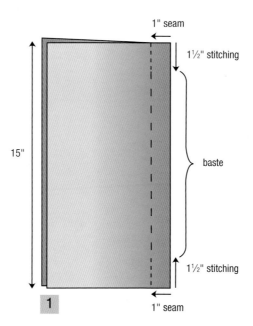

1" seam

1½" stitching

15"

baste

1½" stitching

1

1" seam

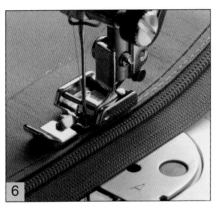

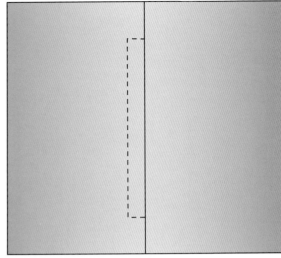

7 Starting at the seamline, topstitch $\frac{1}{2}$" (1.3 cm) across the bottom of the zipper. Pivot and continue stitching $\frac{1}{2}$" (1.3 cm) from the basted seam, along the entire length of the zipper. Pivot at the other end of the zipper, stopping at the seam line. Backstitch. Remove the basting stitches.

5 Attach the zipper foot to your machine. If your machine requires it, change the needle position so the needle is on the left side of the foot. Stitch the right side of the zipper tape to the seam allowance. The line of stitching should be about $\frac{1}{4}$" (6 mm) from the coil.

6 Close the zipper and turn the pillow back right side up. Smooth the seam allowance away from the zipper, forming a fold next to the basting stitches. If necessary, position the needle on the right side of the foot. Stitch along the fold though all thicknesses.

measuring for ruffles

To determine the amount of fabric you need for a ruffled fabric edge, follow these steps:

1. Decide how wide (or deep) you want the ruffle to be, making sure to include the amount of seam allowance you need for the project. Double this measurement (the fabric will be folded in half).

2. To determine the length (or fullness) of the ruffle, measure around the sides of the project and double the measurement. The extra length ensures there will be enough fabric to trim the entire project and enough for the gathers, too.

Making the Ruffle

1 Stitch together the short ends of the bias strips, right sides together, to form one long bias strip. Sew together the short ends of the strip to make one continuous loop. Fold the loop of fabric in half lengthwise, wrong sides together, matching the raw edges. Press lightly.

2 Fold the ruffle into fourths (folding will help you fit the ruffle into the corners of the pillow before gathering). Mark the centers of the folded sections by clipping ³⁄₈" (1 cm) into the seam allowance with a scissors. Work carefully. Don't clip any farther into the seam allowance or you will have a hole in the corner of the finished ruffle.

3 Place the cord about ³⁄₈" (1 cm) from the raw edge of the ruffle. Hold a 4" (10 cm) thread tail behind the presser foot. Stitch over the cord with a wide zigzag stitch, being careful not to catch the cord with the stitches. Stitch around the entire ruffle, leaving a 4" (10 cm) thread tail at the end.

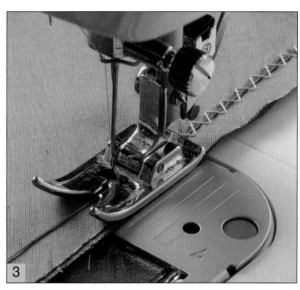

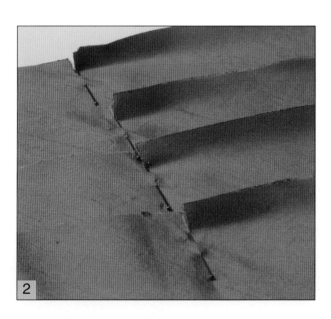

ruffle-edge pillow

To eliminate pointy "dog ears" on the corners of your pillow, make a mark 3¾" (9.5 cm) from each corner of the pillow front. At each corner, mark a point ½" (1.3 cm) from the raw edge. With a fabric pencil or chalk marker, draw a line from the marked points, as shown in the photo. Trim

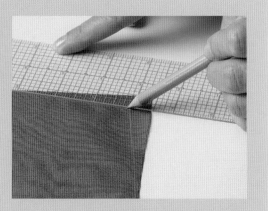

away the fabric along these lines. Repeat the process on the flat piece of the pillow back. After you stitch and turn the pillow right side out, all four corners will have a smooth, even shape.

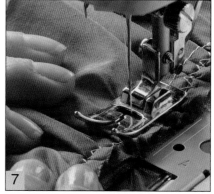

4 Lay the ruffle on the pillow front, right sides together. Match the raw edges and the clip markings to the corners of the pillow front. Pin at the corners, being careful not to pin through the gathering cord.

5 Gently but firmly pull the gathering cord to gather the ruffle on each side of the pillow. Distribute the gathers evenly and round the ruffles slightly at each of the corners. Carefully pin the ruffle edges all around the pillow.

6 With a long, straight stitch, sew the ruffle to the pillow, stitching just inside the gathering row. Remove the pins as you come to them.

7 To finish the pillow, open the zipper. Lay the pillow back on the pillow front, right sides together, matching the raw edges. The ruffle will be sandwiched between the two pieces of fabric. Stitch around the pillow with a $1/2$" (1.3 cm) seam allowance.

8 Turn the pillow right side out through the zipper opening. Slip in the pillow form.

Zip it up,
and you're done!

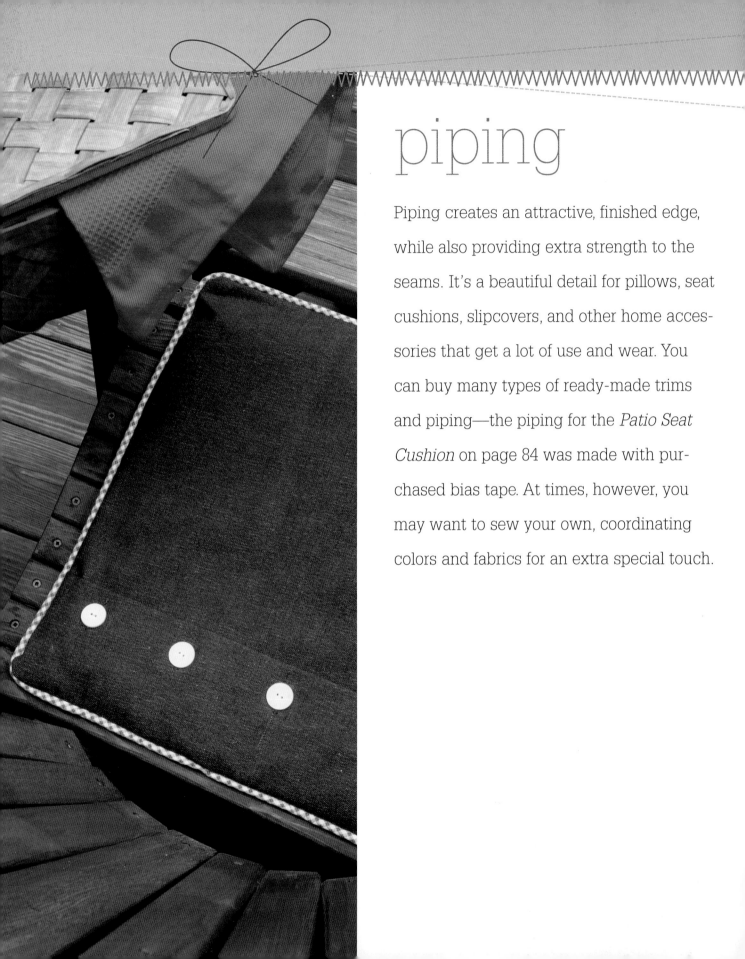

piping

Piping creates an attractive, finished edge, while also providing extra strength to the seams. It's a beautiful detail for pillows, seat cushions, slipcovers, and other home accessories that get a lot of use and wear. You can buy many types of ready-made trims and piping—the piping for the *Patio Seat Cushion* on page 84 was made with purchased bias tape. At times, however, you may want to sew your own, coordinating colors and fabrics for an extra special touch.

Making Piping

Piping is easy to make. You simply cover a length of cord with a long strip of fabric that has been cut on the bias (at a 45-degree angle to the grain). Then machine-stitch to secure the cord inside the fabric. The bias-cut fabric allows the fabric to "stretch" around corners and curves as you assemble your project so you get a better fit.

The overall look of the project will determine the best size for your piping. Smaller, more delicate projects or projects made from lightweight fabrics look best with a thin piping. For larger projects or projects made from heavier or more textured fabrics, a thicker, bolder piping would be a better choice.

The thickness of the filler cord determines the thickness of your piping. It also determines the width of the bias strip you'll need to cover the cord. Wrap a tape measure around the cord, and note the measurement. Triple that measurement, and add $1^{1}/_{4}$" (3.2 cm) for the seam allowances. The total indicates the needed width for the bias strip. For example, for a $^{1}/_{4}$" (6 mm) cord,

the bias strip would need to be 2" (5.1 cm) wide:

Cord $= {}^{1}/_{4}$" (6 mm)
$[{}^{1}/_{4}$" (6 mm) $\times$ 3] $+ 1^{1}/_{4}$" (3.2 cm) = 2" (5.1 cm)

To figure out how long your piping should be, measure around the sides of your project. That measurement indicates the length of cord you'll need—and the length of the bias strip you'll need to make. To this measurement, add at least 1" (2.5 cm) to allow enough fabric to overlap the raw edges.

To cut fabric for the bias strips, work with a ruler and a fabric pencil or chalk marker to mark the true bias of the fabric (page 9). Draw a line parallel to the bias, at a distance equal to the strip width you calculated. (You may have to cut more than one strip to get the total length you need.) Cut out the bias strip, and wrap it around the cording, right side out, matching the raw edges. With a zipper foot, stitch closely alongside the cord to enclose it in the fabric, keeping the raw edges even as you stitch.

Decorative Piping

You can make the bias strips from a fabric that matches or contrasts with your project, depending on the finished look you want. You can also embellish the fabric with decorative stitches and colorful threads to create your own design as for the *Pillow with Rosettes and Decorative Piping* (page 78). If you want to cover the piping with decorative stitches and threads, stitch the surface of the fabric before cutting out the strips and before adding the cord.

Size

14" (35.6 cm) square

Seam Allowance

½" (1.3 cm)

Materials

½ yard (0.45 m) of fabric for pillow
    front and back

1¼ yards (1.14 m) of fabric for rosettes
    and piping

1¾ yards (1.6 m) of ⁶⁄₃₂" (0.4 cm) piping cord

1 yard (0.9 m) or 1 package of lightweight
    tear-away stabilizer

15" × 15" (38.1 × 38.1 cm) low-loft quilt batting
    (to support rosettes on pillow front)

Notions

Marking tools

Pins

All-purpose thread to match pillow fabric

One 12" (30.5 cm) zipper (select a matching
    color zipper)

Cutting tools

Heavy-duty thread or lightweight cord for
    gathering

Variety of decorative threads to embellish
    piping (optional)

Safety pins

One 14" (35.6 cm) square pillow form

Cutting List

For pillow front:
Cut one 15" × 15" (38.1 × 38.1 cm) square.

For pillow back:
Cut two 8½" × 15" (21.6 × 38.1 cm) pieces.

For rosettes:
Cut three 6" × 42" (15.2 × 106.7 cm) bias pieces.

For piping (do not cut until after embellishing
    fabric with decorative stitches):
    Cut 1½" (3.8 cm)-wide bias strips (about
    64" (1.62 m) total length).

pillow with rosettes and decorative piping

This dressy, sophisticated pillow features decorative piping and a centerpiece of three-dimensional fabric rosettes. It was made with two contrasting but complementary fabrics—one for the pillow body and the other for both the rosettes and the piping. The textured piping is embellished with a variety of decorative stitching in a thread color that matches the chocolate-brown pillow fabric.

If you prefer, you can make the entire pillow—rosettes, piping, and all—with a single fabric. Or to create a more casual style, mix prints and solids or checks and plaids. You can even change the size of the rosettes to create a smaller, center cluster—or make enough of them to completely cover the entire pillow front. Let this lovely project bring out the designer in you!

here's a hint!

When embellishing piping, match the thread color to the color of the fabric for a tone-on-tone texture. Choose a thread of a contrasting color to create a bolder surface design.

Inserting the Zipper

1. Place the two pillow back pieces right sides together. With a fabric pencil or chalk marker, draw a line along the length of the fabric, 1" (2.5 cm) from the long raw edge. Make a mark 1½" (3.8 cm) from the top of the line and another mark 1½" (3.8 cm) from the bottom. Pin along the marked line.

2. Sew from the bottom of the fabric until you reach the first 1½" (3.8 cm) mark, back-stitching at the beginning and end of the stitching. Reposition the fabric and sew from the second mark to the top of the fabric, backstitching at the beginning and end.

3. Change the stitch length to the longest stitch (or basting stitch). Machine-baste the unstitched portion of the line. Press open the basted seam.

4. Open the zipper and place it face down on the seam allowance, centered over the basting stitches. The coil of the zipper should rest on the seam line. Attach the right side of the zipper to the seam allowance with pin or a glue stick.

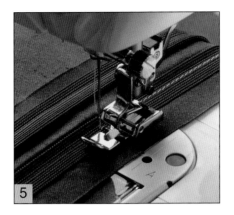

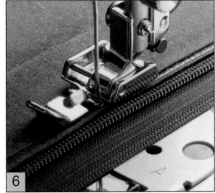

5. Attach the zipper foot to your machine. If your machine requires it, change the needle position so the needle is on the left side of the foot. Stitch the right side of the zipper tape to the seam allowance. The line of stitching should be about ¼" (6 mm) from the coil.

6. Close the zipper, and turn the pillow back right side up. Smooth the seam allowance away from the zipper, forming a fold next to the basting stitches. If necessary, position the needle on the right side of the foot. Stitch along the fold though all thicknesses.

7. Starting at the seamline, topstitch ½" (1.3 cm) across the bottom of the zipper. Pivot and continue stitching ½" (1.3 cm) from the basted seam, along the entire length of the zipper. Pivot at the other end of the zipper, stopping at the seam line. Backstitch. Remove the basting stitches.

8. Trim the corners of the pillow front and back to avoid pointy, "dog-ear" corners (page 38). Make a mark 3¾" (9.5 cm) from each corner of each pillow piece. At each corner, mark a point ½" (1.3 cm) from the raw edge. With a fabric pencil or chalk marker, draw a line from the marked points. Trim away the fabric along these lines.

9. Pin the batting to the wrong side of the pillow front. Machine-baste the batting in place, stitching within the ½" (1.3 cm) seam allowance (so the stitches will not show on the finished pillow front).

Making the Piping

1 First, cut the three bias strips for the rosettes, referring to the cutting list on page 78 and the drawing below. Set aside the strips.

2 Position the tear-away stabilizer on the wrong side of the fabric for the cord, following the manufacturer's instructions. The stabilizer will keep the fabric flat and firm as you stitch the surface.

3 With decorative stitches, embellish enough fabric to cover the two 1½" (3.8 cm)-wide bias strips you need for the cord. Select one or more stitch styles, depending on the look you want. Small stitch patterns will work best around the cord—zigzag, feather stitch, and serpentine, for example. Stitch the rows of decorative stitches on the right side of the fabric, parallel to the lengthwise grain (at a 45-degree angle to the cut edges).

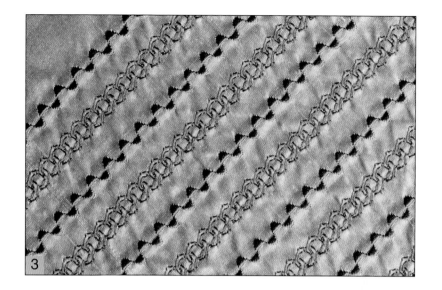

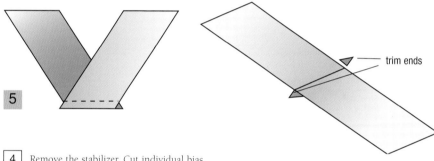

4 Remove the stabilizer. Cut individual bias strips as shown in the drawing at left.

5 You will use 1¾ yards (1.6 m) of piping—so you need a bias strip that is a total of 64" (1.6 m) long. To make a strip that length, join together the two individual bias strips. Join them right sides together, at their short ends, to make one long continuous strip. Offset the ends slightly to align them and trim the points of excess fabric in the seam allowance, as shown in the drawings above.

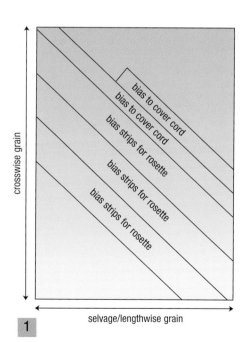

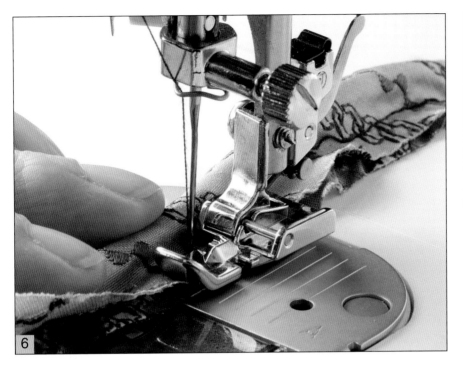

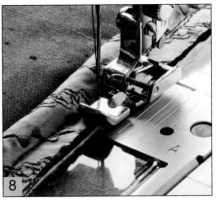

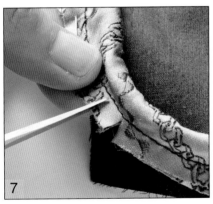

6 Sew the strips together with a straight stitch and a ¼" (6 mm) seam allowance. Press the seams open. Center the cord on the wrong side of the bias strip. Fold the strip over the cord, matching the raw edges. With a zipper foot, stitch closely alongside the cord to enclose it in the fabric, keeping the raw edges even as you stitch.

7 Pin the piping to the right side of the pillow front, aligning the raw edges. Slightly round and ease the piping at the corners. Carefully clip into the seam allowance (avoid clipping into the stitching and the cord) to help the piping lie flat at the corners.

8 Stitch the cording to the right side of the pillow front, matching raw edges. Stitch as close as you can to the piping. Begin and end the stitching about 1½" (3.8 cm) from where the ends of the cord will meet.

9 Trim the cord so the ends meet and stitch them together. Fold the end of the bias strip under about ½" (1.3 cm). Refold the strip over the cord and hand-baste to the pillow front.

10 To finish the pillow, open the zipper. Pin the pillow back and front, right sides together, matching raw edges. The piping will be sandwiched between the pieces. Stitch around the pillow with a ½" (1.3 cm) seam allowance. Turn the pillow right side out through the zipper opening.

here's a hint!

A thicker filler cord will create a bolder piping on the edge of the pillow. If you work with a larger—or a smaller—cord than the size indicated here, be sure to adjust the width of your bias strips accordingly.

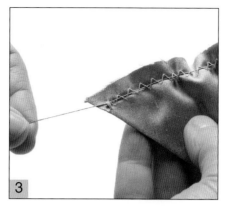

Making the Rosettes

1 To make each of the three rosettes, fold a strip of the rosette bias in half lengthwise, wrong sides together. Gently press with a cool iron. Place the template (page 108) at each end of each strip and trim the fabric to shape.

2 With a zigzag stitch, sew the heavy thread or cording to the right side of the fabric, about ¼" (6 mm) from the raw edge. Leave a 4" (10.2 cm) tail at each end of the stitching. Be sure your zigzag stitch is wide enough so you don't catch the cord in the stitching.

3 Gently pull the gathering cord on each end until the bias strip measures 21" (53.3 cm). Knot the gathering cords to secure them at the ends.

4 To form each rosette, roll the gathered piece, with one end of the strip at the center. Hand-sew the edges together as you form the petals. Stitch the ends together to secure.

5 Arrange the three rosettes on the front of the pillow. Working from the inside of the pillow, secure each by pinning it in place with large safety pins. Hand-sew the rosettes to secure, again working from the inside of the pillow. Remove the safety pins, and insert the pillow form. Zip the zipper.

Find the perfect place to display your new pillow.

Size
17" × 18" (43.2 × 45.7 cm)

Seam Allowance
½" (1.3 cm)

Materials
⅔ yard (0.6 m) heavyweight fabric, such as
    denim or canvas

Notions
Pins
Matching all-purpose thread
Cutting tools
Liquid seam sealant
One package of extra-wide double-fold bias tape
2 yards (1.8 m) of ³⁄₁₆" (0.4 cm) piping cord
Denim or heavy-duty sewing-machine needle
One 15" × 17" × 1" (38.1 × 43.2 × 2.5 cm)
    seat cushion pad
Five matching buttons

Cutting List
From fabric:
Cut one 17" × 19" (43.2 × 48.3 cm) for the back.
Cut one 15½" × 19" (39.4 × 48.3 cm) for one
    section of the front.
Cut one 6½" × 19" (16.5 × 48.3 cm) for the
    other section of the front.

Note: Contrasting thread is used in the
photographs for visibility.

patio seat cushion

Pull up a seat—just about anywhere! This seat cushion is a cheerful and durable addition to your porch, deck, or patio furniture. It's also great to have one or more extra on hand in case unexpected guests arrive to join in the fun. You can toss these cushions on the lawn, on the beach, or on a bench by the pool. You make the piping with packaged bias tape, so you'll get professional-looking piping in half the time. So, make just one or make several—in colorful matching or contrasting fabrics. The instructions here are for one seat cushion.

1 To make the cushion front, turn under one long edge of the large front piece 1¼" (3.2 cm). Press and stitch in place. Turn under one long edge of the smaller front piece 1¼" (3.2 cm) and press. Stitch in place.

2 Make five evenly spaced buttonholes in the smaller piece. (Check your machine manual if you need help and to be sure you use the correct foot and machine settings.)

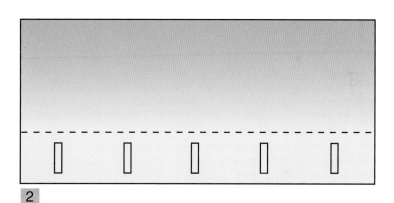

2

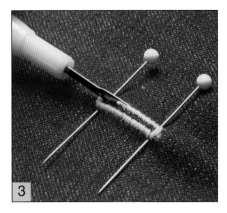

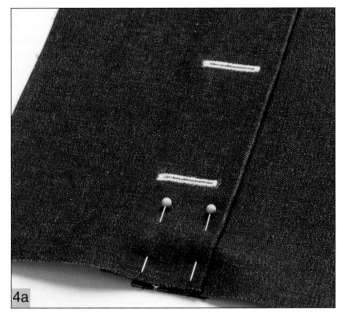

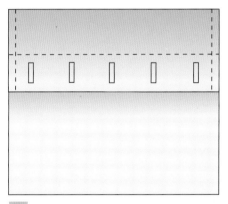

3 Now open the buttonholes. Insert straight pins at each end of the buttonhole. The pins will prevent you from accidentally cutting through the bar tacks (the stitching at each end) and into the fabric. Insert the blade of the seam ripper (or the point of a small, sharp scissors) into the center of the buttonhole. Carefully cut toward one end, then turn the work and cut toward the other end. You can apply liquid seam sealant to the cut edges to strengthen them and prevent raveling.

4 Pin the two front pieces together, right sides up. The piece with the buttonholes should lie on top of the larger piece. Together, they form the top of the seat cushion, which measures 17" × 19" (43.2 × 48.3 cm).

With the general purpose foot, sew together the overlapping sections, stitching in the seam allowances at the edges, as shown in the drawing.

liquid seam sealant

Seam sealant is a clear liquid that keeps threads from unraveling. You can use it to reinforce the ends of a buttonhole before you cut out the opening—but be sure you allow the sealant to dry completely before you cut. After the sealant has been applied, it creates a permanent finish that can be washed or dry-cleaned. Use it sparingly, and read the product instructions carefully.

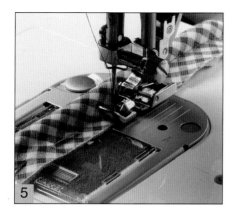

5 Press open the bias tape so that it lies flat. Center the cord on the bias tape and fold the tape over the cord, matching raw edges. Pin in place. Attach the zipper foot and change the needle position, if necessary, so the needle is on the left side of the zipper foot. Stitch close to the cord.

6 Pin the piping to the right side of the cushion bottom, aligning the raw edges. Slightly round and ease the piping at the corners. Sew the piping around the fabric with a $\frac{1}{2}$" (1.3 cm) seam allowance. Stop stitching $1\frac{1}{2}$" (3.8 cm) from where the ends of the cording will meet.

7 Cut off one end of the cord so that it overlaps the other cord. Fold under $\frac{1}{2}$" (1.3 cm) of the overlapping bias strip. Fold it around the other end and finish stitching.

8 Pin together the right sides of the cushion top and bottom. With the zipper foot, stitch around the cushion through all thicknesses. Clip the corners to reduce fabric bulk. Turn the cushion right side out. Sew on the buttons by hand.

Insert the chair pad and button it up.

easy quilting

Quilts are made up of a top piece of fabric, batting (or filler), and the bottom piece of fabric (or backing). To quilt, you stitch through all three layers to create a three-dimensional, textured surface. Before you quilt, however, you need to assemble the top piece of fabric—which you can do in several ways.

Quilting Basics

Making quilt tops—especially patch-work quilt tops—is like making a puzzle. You assemble the fabric pieces in a logical sequence to create the design. To be sure the pieces will fit together neatly, you must make sure they are exactly the right size. Accurate cutting and sewing are the first rules of quilting. A small error can multiply quickly, so double-check your work as you go.

Some of the tools you'll need are a rotary cutter and mat, a fabric pencil or chalk marker, and a good quilting ruler (a transparent ruler with clear markings).

In quilting, you generally work with a $\frac{1}{4}$" (6 mm) seam allowance. Check to see if your machine has a $\frac{1}{4}$" (6 mm) foot, which is also called a patchwork foot. Most of these feet are designed so that the sides of the foot are $\frac{1}{4}$" (6 mm) away from the needle. This design makes it easy to line up the raw edges of the fabric with the edge of the foot to stitch a perfect seam allowance. Some $\frac{1}{4}$" (6 mm) feet may have a slightly different design, so be sure to test the foot by stitch-ing a piece of scrap fabric. If you don't have a $\frac{1}{4}$" (6 mm) foot, mark the needle plate to make your own guide (page 25).

Three Quilting Techniques

There are several fun and versatile quilting styles that you can use for home accents. The *Sunny Table Runner* (page 90) is made with patchwork techniques. Patchwork is made simply by joining together small pieces of fabric to create a larger design. The *Cafe Mocha Wall Hanging* (page 96) includes a tech-nique called appliqué. In appliqué, you sew small pieces of fabric onto a larger piece of fabric to form designs, pictures, or words. The *Flower Petal Table Topper* (page 104) is made with a technique called free-motion quilting, or stippling. When free-motion quilting, you manually guide the fabric as you stitch to create a textured design.

Size

22" × 58" (55.9 × 147.3 cm)

Seam Allowance

¼" (6 mm)

Materials

For the Rail Fence blocks:

¼ yard (0.23 m) each of three coordinating
   yellow fabrics

¼ yard (0.23 m) each of three coordinating navy
   blue print fabrics

⅛ yard (0.11 m) each of three coordinating
   medium to light blue fabrics

For the border:

⅓ yard (0.3 m) of navy blue print fabric

For the backing:

1⅔ yards (1.52 m) of navy print fabric

⅔ yard (0.6 m) of 60" (152 cm)-wide low-loft
   cotton batting

Notions

Long quilter's pins

Rotary cutting tools

Ruler

All-purpose thread

Monofilament thread

All-purpose or cotton thread to match the
   backing fabric

Fabric spray adhesive

Fabric tape

Marking tools

Cutting List

Note: WOF stands for "width of fabric" (page 8).

Cut two 2½" (6.4 cm) wide × WOF strips of
   each of the three yellow fabrics.

Cut two 2½" (6.4 cm) wide × WOF strips of
   each of the three navy fabrics.

Cut one 2½" (6.4 cm) wide × WOF strips of
   each of three medium blue print fabrics.

Cut 24" × 60" (61 × 152.4 cm) piece of cotton
   batting.

Cut 22" × 58" (55.9 × 147.3 cm) piece of
   backing fabric.

Cut four 2½" (6.4 cm) wide × WOF pieces of
   the navy border fabric.

sunny table runner

This bright and cheerful table runner is a great first quilting project. You'll learn the classic Rail Fence block pattern and the basic steps for piecing geometric shapes. Change the fabric colors to suit your taste or match your room's color scheme. You can use the same techniques to make matching placemats, too. Work with cotton quilting fabrics (which are 42" to 45" [106.7 to 114.3 cm] wide), but preshrink them before you start so that the finished runner won't shrink after you wash it.

When making this project, you will press some seams open to reduce bulk because the project will sit on a tabletop. Others are pressed to one side—so the darker fabric doesn't show on the right side of the project.

 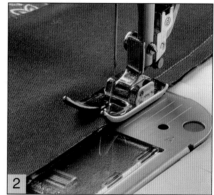

Making the Blocks

1 With right sides together, match the raw edges of two yellow strips. Pin and sew along the length of the strips, with an accurate $\frac{1}{4}$" (6 mm) seam allowance. Position a third yellow strip alongside one of the others, right sides together, to form a rectangular block. Pin and sew. Press the seams open. Repeat to create a second block with the remaining three yellow strips.

2 Repeat step 1 with the strips of the navy blue fabrics and the strips of the medium to light blue fabrics.

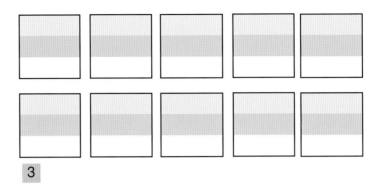

3

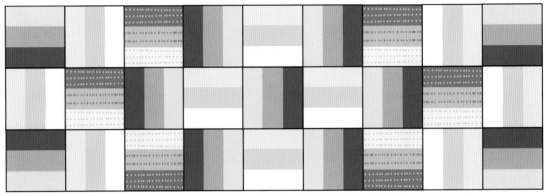

4

3 | Cut the rectangular blocks to make ten 6½" (16.5 cm) squares of yellow, eleven squares of navy, and six squares of light blue.

4 | Working on a large, flat surface, arrange the blocks as shown in the drawing to form the traditional Rail Fence pattern. There are three rows in the pattern. Start by laying out the bottom row, noting the block color and the direction of the pieced strips.

5 | Now stitch the blocks together, sewing one row at a time. Start with the first two blocks at one end of the bottom row. Pin the blocks right sides together and sew—don't forget your ¼" (6 mm) seam allowance! Continue to add the blocks of the first row to form a long strip. Check the drawing for the correct sequence. If you make a mistake, get out your seam ripper and fix it right away—if you piece out of sequence, your entire pattern will be off. Continue pinning and sewing until you have pieced all three rows.

6 | Lay the three rows on your work surface in the correct order, following drawing 4. Press all the bottom row seams to the left. Press all the center row seams to the right. Press all the top row seams to the left.

here's a hint!

Most quilters piece fabrics with a neutral color thread that will blend with the colors of the fabrics. Choose a white or light grey for light or pastel fabrics, a medium grey or tan for medium fabrics, and a dark grey for dark fabrics. For the quilting itself, the choice of thread and thread color is up to you!

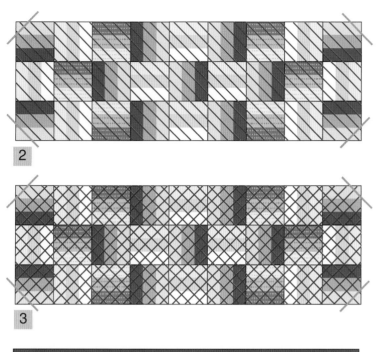

2

3

5

Making the Patchwork Top

1 With right sides together, stitch the three rows together, making sure the individual blocks in each adjacent row align.

2 Secure the quilt top to a flat work surface with tape, keeping the fabric taut and smooth. With the chalk and ruler, mark diagonal lines 2" (5.1 cm) apart on the patchwork top. Mark each of the corners with a short diagonal line, as shown in the drawing.

3 Mark diagonal lines across the fabric in the opposite direction at 2" (5.1 cm) intervals.

4 Match the 2½" (6.4 cm) raw edges of the four navy border strips, right sides together, and sew to form one long strip. Press the seams open.

5 With right sides together, place the border strip along one long edge of the patchwork top, aligning one raw edge of the strip with the raw edge of the patchwork. Pin and sew. Press the seam toward the border. Trim the end of the border strip so it is flush with the other raw edge of the quilt top.

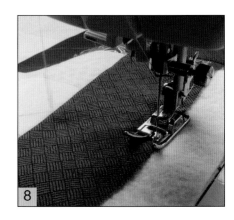

6 Add a border to the other long side of the quilt top in the same way. Trim the end of the strip to align with the edge of the quilt top. Press the seam toward the border strip.

7 Add a border to each of the short edges of the quilt top in the same way.

8 Following the manufacturer's directions, spray the batting with fabric spray adhesive. Place the wrong side of the quilt top onto the cotton batting. Set a long stitch length to machine-baste a scant $1/4$" (6 mm) seam (scant means "a little less than") from the outside edge of the pieced top. Trim the excess batting close to the raw edge of the pieced top.

9 With right sides together and raw edges matching, pin the quilt backing to the batting/pieced top. Set your machine for a medium-stitch length. Attach the even-feed presser foot, if your machine has one—if not, stitch with the general purpose foot. Join the backing to the top by sewing around all sides with a $1/4$" (6 mm) seam allowance. Leave a 9" (22.9 cm) opening on one of the long sides of the table runner.

10 To eliminate bulk, trim the corners at an angle. Turn the table runner right side out through the opening. Stitch the opening closed and press the edges of your runner.

quilting with a walking foot

A walking foot (also called an even-feed foot) is a helpful accessory for machine-quilting. The walking foot works like another set of feed dogs—on top of the fabric. The foot and the machine's feed dogs work together to pull the fabric layers evenly along the machine bed as you quilt so that your stitches will be even and consistent.

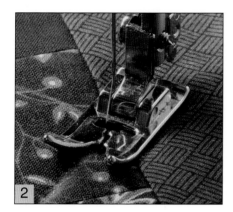

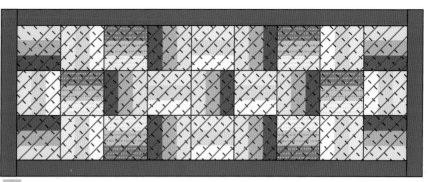

Machine-Quilting

1 | Thread the machine with monofilament thread. Wind the bobbin with navy thread or thread that matches the backing fabric. Attach the walking foot, if you have one. If not, quilt with a general-purpose presser foot.

2 | Position the patchwork top under the presser foot, aligning the needle with the end of the diagonal line in one of the corners. Instead of backstitching, begin the quilting by taking several very short stitches to secure the stitching. Change the setting for a medium stitch length, and continue stitching the full length of the marked line. If you have pinned the fabric layers, remove the pins as you come to them. Take a few very short stitches to end the stitching. Cut the top and bottom threads.

3 | Reposition the fabric to align the needle with the end of the next diagonal line. Continue stitching all the parallel diagonal lines in that direction in the same way.

4 | Turn the table runner and quilt all the parallel diagonal lines in that direction, following the same process described in Step 2.

5 | Working on the right side of the quilt, stitch along the seams that join the border strips to the patchwork blocks. This type of stitching is called "stitching in the ditch," because the stitches are hidden in the seam. The stitches will emphasize the pieced portion of the design. Be sure to begin and end the stitching with several very short stitches to secure it.

6 | To finish, topstitch around the edge of the table runner with a ¼" (6 mm) seam allowance.

here's a hint!

Pins will help keep the fabric layers from shifting as you quilt. Pin together the layers with the quilter's pins, spacing the pins every 6 to 8" (15 to 20 cm). Remember, you will be stitching on the chalk lines, so try not to pin in those areas.

Size
20" × 23½" (50.8 × 59.7 cm)

Seam Allowance
¼" (0.6 cm)

Materials
Note: Work with 45" (114.3 cm) wide cotton quilting fabrics.

½ yard (0.45 m) of green fabric
1 yard (0.9 m) of gold fabric
⅛ yard (0.11m) of rust fabric
¼ yard (0.23 m) of purple fabric
¼ yard (0.23 m) of black fabric, for border,
        binding, and letters
Scrap of batik or marble print, for trails of steam
Scrap of brown stripe, for outside of coffee cup
Scrap of dark brown, for inside of coffee cup
21" × 25" (53.3 cm × 63.5 cm) low-loft cotton batting
Double-sided fusible web

Notions
Rotary cutting tools
All-purpose thread for piecing
Monofilament thread or threads to match fabrics
Machine-embroidery threads for appliqué (optional)
Pins
1" (2.5 cm) safety pins
Fabric spray adhesive (optional)
Marking tools
1" (2.5 cm) bias tape maker (optional)

Note: Contrasting thread is used in the
photographs for visibility.

café mocha wall hanging

Give your kitchen or breakfast nook a cozy, "coffee house" feel with this cute wall decoration. You can change the lettering, rearrange the motifs, or alter the color scheme to create your own variation on the theme!

Appliqué is a fun and versatile quilting technique. Each of the shapes is drawn on the paper side of fusible web, traced onto fabric, and stitched in place. The templates for the shapes for this project are on page 109—but with a little imagination, you can design and draw your own appliqués to create a bit of personal flair. The wall hanging features an edge binding that finishes the frame.

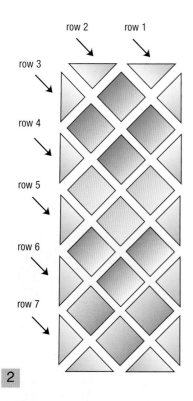

1 Cut seven of the 2½" (6.4 cm) green squares in half, diagonally, creating 14 triangles.

2 On a flat surface, lay out the green triangles and the 2¼" (5.7 cm) squares of purple, gold, rust, and black as shown in the drawing. You will have seven diagonal rows.

café mocha wall hanging

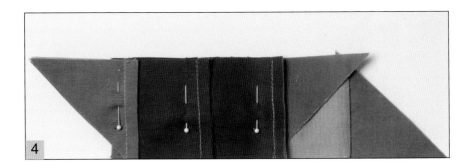

3 | Sew together the triangles and squares in each row, leaving a $^{1}/_{4}$" (6 mm) seam allowance. Press the seams in the same direction in each row, alternating the direction from one row to the next.

4 | Sew together rows 1 and 2, matching the seams. Continue to sew the remaining rows together in the same way, to make one large pieced block.

5 | Sew the large green rectangle to the right edge of the pieced block with a $^{1}/_{4}$" (6 mm) seam allowance. Press the seams toward the green fabric. Sew the $2^{1}/_{4}$" (5.7 cm) green strip to the bottom edge of this piece. Press.

6 | Sew the $1^{1}/_{2}$" (3.8 cm) green strip to the top edge of the piece. Press. Trim away the excess strip fabric.

7 | Sew the excess green strip fabric to the left edge of the piece. Press and trim away any excess fabric.

8 | Cut the 8" (20.3 cm) gold square in half diagonally. Cut the $6^{1}/_{2}$" (16.5 cm) purple square in half diagonally. Sew the purple triangles to the short edges of one of the gold triangles. The purple triangles will overlap at their points. (You won't need the other gold triangle—save it for another project.)

squaring up

The fabric may stretch somewhat as you assemble the rows, so you may have to "square up" the pieced block. Lay the block on a gridded cutting mat. Lay the straightedge ruler over the corners and sides of the block, and trim away any excess or uneven edges

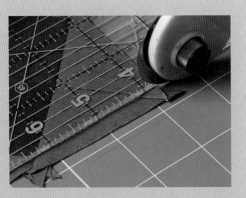

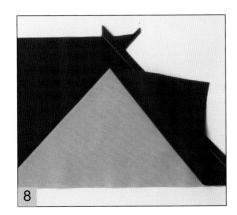

with the rotary cutter (see page 15). Check the block after finishing each step of the assembly—and square up again whenever necessary.

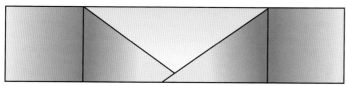

9

9   Sew the 4" × 6" (10.2 × 15.2 cm) purple rectangles to the sides of the assembled piece, as shown in the drawing.

10   Sew the purple/gold section to the bottom edge of the green section to create the central design of the wall hanging.

11   Cut the black border strips in lengths equal to the length of the top, sides, and bottom of the wall hanging. Sew the border strips to the top and bottom edges, right sides together. Press the seams toward the border.

12   Sew the four remaining 2½" (6.4 cm) colored squares to the ends of the side border pieces. Carefully match and pin seams before you stitch.

13   Sew the borders to the side edges of the wall hanging, matching seams. Press the seams toward the border.

Making the Appliqué Shapes

1   The templates for the cup, the inside of the cup, the letters, and the wisps of steam are on page 109. Trace the templates onto the paper side of the double-sided fusible web. The templates are already reversed so the pieces will "read" on the right side when stitched to the wall hanging.

2   Following the manufacturer's recommendations, apply the web fusing to the wrong side of the appliqué fabrics for each shape. Cut out the shapes, peel off paper, and position all the appliqués except the wisps of steam (you'll apply those later). Follow the photograph on page 96 for placement.

3   Fuse the shapes to the surface of the wall hanging. Place tear-away stabilizer on the wrong side of the wall hanging in those areas where you will appliqué to keep the stitches from distorting the fabric.

5

4   Thread the needle with all-purpose, rayon, or decorative thread. Begin stitching the appliqué with a straight stitch or very narrow zigzag, right along the edge, to help hold the shape in place as you sew.

5   Stitch a satin stitch around each shape, enclosing the raw edges, as described on page 44. To make smooth corners and curves, stop sewing when the needle is in the fabric, lift the presser foot, and pivot the fabric very slightly before you continue sewing. When you have stitched all the appliqués, remove the tear-away stabilizer from the wrong side of the wall hanging.

fusible web

Fusible web is a manufactured fiber that melts slightly when heated. It allows you to fuse one fabric to another by applying heat with an iron. Fusible web is backed with paper, so you can trace or draw shapes and patterns directly on it and cut them out. After the appliqué shape is fused to the fabric, you can easily stitch around it—without having to worry about pinning or holding it in place.

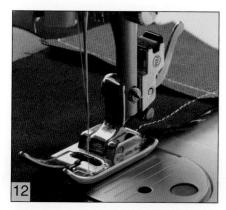

12

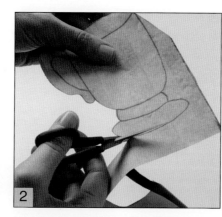

2

Channel Quilting

1 Lay the backing fabric on a flat surface, right side down. Lay the batting on top of the backing. Lay the wall hanging on top of the batting, right side up. Secure the three layers with safety pins or fabric spray adhesive.

2 With chalk and a ruler, draw a wide zigzag line along the long edge of the green fabric, starting about ½" (1.3 cm) away from the edges of the colored boxes at upper left. Mark parallel lines ½" (1.3 cm) apart along the entire surface of the green fabric. These lines will help guide you as you quilt a chevron-style pattern. Quilting in evenly spaced parallel rows—in any direction—is called channel quilting.

3 Thread the machine with green thread in the needle and gold thread in the bobbin. (Or you can use monofilament instead). Attach the walking foot, if your machine has one (page 94). If not, quilt with your general-purpose foot. Position the needle on the marked line closest to the edge of the green fabric. Stitch from the center of the line to the outer edges of the wall hanging.

4 Begin the quilting by taking several very short straight stitches to secure the ends. Adjust the setting for a medium stitch length and stitch along the rest of the line. Take a few very short stitches to end and cut the top and bottom threads. Reposition the fabric to align the needle with the center of the next zigzag line. Continue to fill in the green background fabric with lines of stitching. Start and stop the stitching at the tops and bottoms of the letters.

5 Thread the machine with a thread that matches or contrasts with the gold triangle. Mark diagonal lines within the gold triangle, spaced about ½" (1.3 cm) apart and parallel to the edges of the triangle. Stitch along these lines to quilt the fabric.

6 Thread the machine with a thread that matches or contrasts with the purple fabric. Mark parallel lines about 1½" (3.8 cm) apart within the purple areas of the wall hanging. The intersecting lines should be parallel to the bottom and side edges.

7 When you've finished quilting, check that the fabric is still "square." The shape may have become slightly distorted while you were quilting. Square up the edges of the border if necessary, as shown on page 98.

here's a hint!

When channel quilting, instead of marking all the parallel lines with chalk, you can mark just one line and stitch the others with the help of a stitching or seam guide attachment. Check your instruction manual to find the correct way to attach the guide to your machine. Adjust the guide so that it is ½" (1.3 cm) away from the needle. After you stitch your first drawn line, simply align the guide with that row of stitching to stitch the next row at the correct distance from the first. Continue stitching, each time aligning the guide with the previous row of stitching.

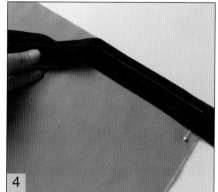

Adding the Binding

1 Sew the three black binding strips together to create one long strip (page 81). Overlap the ends and stitch on the diagonal to join them. Press and fold the long strip in half lengthwise, matching the raw edges. Working with the rotary cutter, mat, and ruler, cut one end of the binding strip at a 45-degree angle.

2 Thread the sewing machine with all-purpose thread to match the binding fabric. Wind the bobbin with the same thread.

3 Working on the right side of the backing, place a pin in one corner of the wall hanging, ¹/₂" (1.3 cm) from one edge. Place another pin ¹/₂" (1.3 cm) from the adjacent edge. Place pins in the other three corners in the same way.

4 Unfold one long edge of the binding strip. Position the unfolded, angled end of the strip at the center of one edge of the backing. Pin the binding strip along the edge to one corner, matching raw edges. Leave 6" (15.2 cm) of the angled end free, and stitch to the first pin at the corner, with a scant ¹/₂" (1.3 cm) seam allowance. Backstitch and remove the fabric from the machine.

bias tape maker

Bias tape makes a great binding to finish and frame your projects. You can buy commercial bias tape, which has neatly folded edges for enclosing raw edges. Or you can make your own, in whatever fabric color or pattern you choose.

A bias tape maker is a handy tool, available in various sizes, depending on the finished width you need for your project. Cut bias strips of fabric (at a 45-degree angle to the grain) that are twice the finished width you want. Feed the strip through the wide end of the bias tape maker, and pull it gently through the narrow end. Finger-press the folds as you pull the tape. When you have pulled the entire length through, press the folds gently with an iron. Your tape is ready to use.

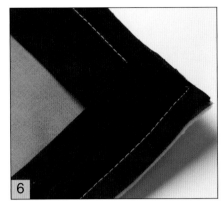

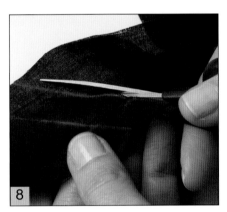

5 Place a pin in the binding 1" (2.5 cm) from the point at which you stopped sewing. Rotate the quilt 90 degrees. Place the pin in the binding right on top of the pin along the edge of the corner, mitering the corners. Reposition the fabric, and begin sewing at the corner. Sew to the next pin, backstitch, and remove the fabric from the machine.

6 Repeat step 5 for each of the remaining corners. Stop sewing 6" (15.2 cm) from the starting point. Backstitch and remove the fabric from the machine.

7 Lay the square end of the binding strip along the edge of the backing fabric. Lay the other, angled end of the strip on top of it. With a ruler and chalk, mark a line on the binding that follows the angled edge. Mark a parallel line ½" (1.3 cm) beyond the first line.

8 Lift the angled end and cut the binding along the first line.

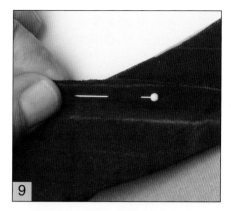

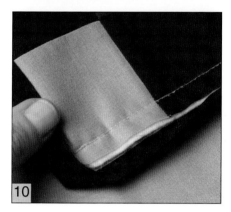

9   With right sides together, bring the binding ends together. Pin and then sew a $1/4$" (6 mm) seam. Press the seam open and finish sewing the binding to the backing.

10   Fold the edges of the binding to the front of the quilt, mitering the corners. Turn the folded edge over to cover the line of stitching and press.

11   To finish the wall hanging, wind the bobbin with all-purpose thread in a color that matches the binding. Pin the binding in place. Topstitch close to the edge of the binding on the right side of the wall hanging.

12   You can hang your wall hanging however you'd like, wherever you'd like. You can stitch on Velcro strips or squares, for example, or you can hang it with a dowel and a length of cord.

To hold the dowel, you'll need a rod pocket on the back. Press under $1/4$" (6 mm) on both short ends and one long edge of the $2^1/2$" × 20" (6.4 × 50.8 cm) rod pocket piece. Place the long raw edge even with the top edge of the wall hanging, wrong side of the pocket to right side of backing. Pin in place. Hand-sew the pressed edge to the backing to form a pocket. Slide the dowel in place. Tie cord to each end.

here's a hint

Most machines have lines on the needle plate or bobbin case cover that indicate seam allowances of various widths. If your machine doesn't, measure $1/4$" (6 mm) from the needle and mark the spot with a strip of tape.

Hang your quilt
and pour yourself
a cup!

Size

17" × 17" (43.2 × 43.2 cm)

Materials

18" (45.7 cm) square of fabric, for top

18" (45.7 cm) square of fabric, for backing

18" (45.7 cm) square of low-loft quilt batting

18" (45.7 cm) square of tulle (to match top
   fabric and flower petals)

Notions

Monofilament thread (clear or smoke, to blend
   with fabrics)

All-purpose sewing thread to match fabric

Fabric spray adhesive

Long quilter's pins

Free-motion (darning/embroidery) foot

Cutting tools

Hand-sewing needle

Small clear plastic beads with holes

Silk flower petals (purchase by the box at
   craft stores or remove individual flowers
   from a silk flower stem)

Note: Contrasting thread is used in the
photographs for visibility.

flower petal table topper

Do you have a favorite flower? Why not enjoy it every day in every season by showcasing it on a tabletop? The silk flowers in this piece were quilted into the fabric with a free-motion quilting technique called stippling—in which you guide the fabric manually as you stitch lines to create a decorative, three-dimensional effect. Because the stippling was done with invisible thread, the stitching doesn't show, but instead creates a wonderful, subtle texture.

Choose fabric and flower colors that closely match for a delicate effect or work with contrasting colors to emphasize the decorative stitching. You can modify these instructions to make a pillow front or a set of placemats, too.

This is a great first project for learning free-motion quilting, which you can also use to create monograms and other embroidered designs. Free-motion quilting takes a little bit of practice, but once you get the hang of it, you'll love this versatile and creative technique.

flower petal table topper

1 Thread the machine with monofilament thread. Wind the bobbin with all-purpose thread in a color matching the top fabric.

2 Spray the wrong side of the top fabric with fabric adhesive, following the manufacturer's instructions. Lay the top fabric on the batting, and smooth in place.

3 Lightly press the flowers with a cool iron. Scatter the flowers randomly over the top fabric.

4 Lay the tulle over the flower petals and fabric. Pin the layers together to secure them for stitching.

5 Lower or cover the feed dogs on your machine. (Some machines have a switch and others have a cover plate. Refer to your machine manual for your specific instructions). Attach your free-motion (darning/embroidery) foot.

doodling by machine

Before you begin free-motion quilting, or any type of quilting, it's always a good idea to warm up. Think of this step as "doodling" with your sewing machine instead of a pen or pencil.

Prepare a "quilt sandwich" with two fabric squares and a square of batting that are the same size—and at least 12" (30.5 cm). Lay the backing right side down. Place the batting on top, and then place the top fabric on the batting, right side up. Pin the layers or use spray adhesive to keep them together. Then, sit down at the machine and doodle away!

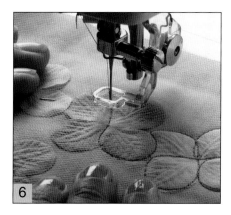

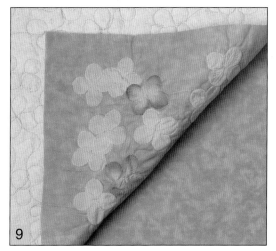

6 Slowly stitch around the flower petals through all the quilt layers. Because the thread is clear, the stitching will seem to disappear into the work, while at the same time creating a three-dimensional effect. Hold the fabric lightly in your hands as you move the fabric around on the machine bed. Continue stippling around the petals until they are all securely attached beneath the tulle.

7 When have finished stitching, lightly press the top of the fabric, using a cool iron so as not to damage the nylon monofilament.

8 Remove the free-motion foot and raise or uncover the feed dogs. Attach a general-purpose or walking foot (see page 94).

9 Position the stippled fabric and bottom fabric right sides together. Stitch all around the piece with a $1/2$" (1.3 cm) seam allowance, leaving a 4" (10.2 cm) area free for turning the work right side out. Clip the corners. Turn the work right side out and press with a cool iron. Hand-stitch the opening closed.

10 Lay a few extra flower petals on the surface of the table topper, but leave the center area free for a centerpiece of your choice. Pin the flowers in place.

With a needle and thread, hand-sew a small bead into the center of each flower, stitching through all the layers of fabric. This decorative stitching not only secures the flowers and all the quilt layers, it adds a little bit of sparkle to the finished piece.

Enjoy your
tabletop blooms
    all year round!

free-motion quilting

Some machines include a free-motion foot (also called a darning/embroidery foot). The foot has a small hole, through which the needle moves up and down (as shown in photo 6). When the needle is down, the foot briefly comes in contact with the surface of the fabric and holds it in place while the stitch is formed. When the needle rises, so does the foot, allowing you to move the fabric to a new position. All this happens very quickly as you stitch.

The machine does not guide the fabric at all when you are free-motion quilting. Instead, you move the fabric yourself, guiding it below the needle to stitch in the areas you choose. If you're just learning, it's a good to idea to work at a slightly slower speed, until you get the feel for it. The speed at which you move the fabric and the speed at which you are sewing determine the look of the stitch.

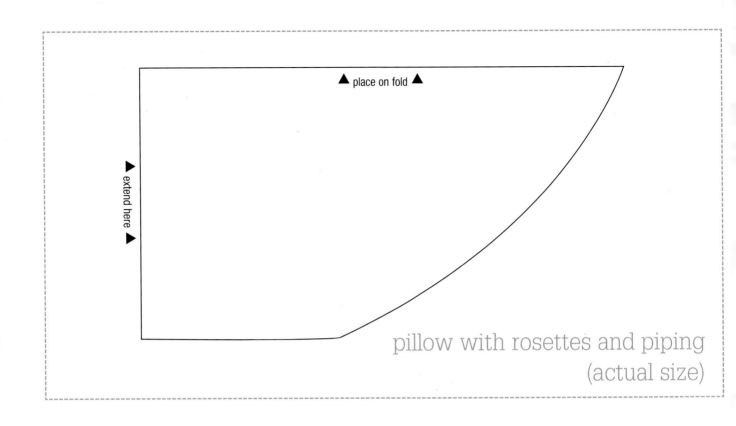

▲ place on fold ▲

▶ extend here ▶

pillow with rosettes and piping
(actual size)

drawstring bag
(actual size)

café mocha wall hanging
enlarge 150%

Creative Publishing
international

Copyright 2007
Creative Publishing international
18705 Lake Drive East
Chanhassen, MN 55317
1-800-328-3895
www.creativepub.com
All rights reserved

President/CEO: Ken Fund
Vice President/Sales & Marketing: Peter Ackroyd
Publisher: Winnie Prentiss

Executive Managing Editor: Barbara Harold
Acquisition Editor: Deborah Cannarella
Associate Editor: Kate Perri
Development Editor: Sharon Boerbon Hanson
Photo Stylist: Joanne Wawra
Senior Design Manager: Brad Springer
Photographers: Robert A. Lisak, Peter Caley
Production Manager: Linda Halls
Cover and Book Design: Mary Rohl
Page Layout: Lois Stanfield
Illustration: Deborah Pierce

Library of Congress Cataloging-in-Publication Data
Hanson, Becky.
  Pattern-free home accents : 15 easy sew projects that build
skills, too / Becky Hanson.
      p. cm. -- (Easy Singer style)
Includes index.
  ISBN-13: 978-1-58923-320-1 (soft cover)
  ISBN-10: 1-58923-320-4 (soft cover)
1. House furnishings. 2. Machine sewing. I. Creative
Publishing International. II. Title. III. Series.
  TT387.H36 2007
  646.2'1--dc22   2006034145

Printed in China
10 9 8 7 6 5 4 3 2 1

acknowledgments

Special thanks to Sharon Hughes, Marleen Baker, and Jeanine
Jones for their contributions

about the author

Becky Hanson received her first sewing machine at age nine,
and she has been sewing ever since. For many years, she represented
the Singer Sewing Company as an education consultant, and she
is now the company's education manager. Becky is the creator and
host of a new series of instructional DVDs for SINGER machines.
She has also designed a series of hands-on sewing events for
machine sewers and has represented Singer Sewing Company
on sewing-education programs on cable television. At home,
Becky creates couture millinery, a craft she studied at the
London College of Fashion in London, England.

suppliers

Coats and Clark
4135 South Stream Blvd.
Charlotte, NC 28277
704-329-5800
www.coatsna.com

Fabric Traditions
1350 Broadway, Suite 2106
New York, NY 10018
212-279-5710
www.fabrictraditions.com

Hancock Fabrics Inc.
One Fashion Way
Baldwyn, MS 38826
877-322-7427
www.hancockfabrics.com

Jo-Ann Fabric and Craft Stores
5555 Darrow Rd.
Hudson, OH 44236
888-739-4120
www.joann.com

Marcus Brothers Textiles Inc.
980 Avenue of the Americas
New York, NY 10018
212-354-8700
www.marcusbrothers.com

Robert Kaufman Fabrics
Box 59266, Greenmead Station
Los Angeles, CA 90059-0266
www.robertkaufman.com

Robison Anton Textile
Company
175 Bergen Blvd.
Fairview, NJ 07022
800-932-0250
www.robison-anton.com

Singer Sewing Company
1224 Heil Quaker Blvd.
LaVergne, TN 37086
615-213-0880
www.singerco.com
*SINGER sewing machines
are available at authorized
SINGER retailers.*

Sulky of America
980 Cobb Place Blvd., Suite 130
Kennesaw, GA 30144
800-874-4115
www.sulky.com

Wrights
85 South St.
West Warren, MA 01092
413-436-7732
www.wrights.com

YLI Corporation
1439 Dave Lyle Blvd., #16C
Rock Hill, SC 29730
803-985-3100
www.ylicorp.com

index